NEW PATHS
THROUGH OLD PALESTINE

Instead of the soft-footed camels, the motor truck stood at the gates of the Holy City.

New Paths
Through Old Palestine

BY
MARGARET SLATTERY

WILDSIDE PRESS

TO

𝔚. 𝔅. 𝔥.

THE UNDERSTANDING COMPANION
OF THE PILGRIMAGE

A WORD ABOUT THE NEW PATHS

From our earliest childhood when at Christmas time we gazed with intense interest at the Wise-men on their gaily caparisoned camels, those great awkward ships of the desert have been associated in our minds with Palestine. The Child held close in Mary's arms as she sat upon the donkey while Joseph urged it on through the day and the night in the hurried flight into Egypt has made that faithful little beast a part of Palestine.

We saw both the donkeys with loaded panniers driven along by wandering Arabs and the strings of camels, soft-footed, heads held proudly high, moving off over the yellow sands up to the hills. But we sat in a modern train, with comfortable leather seats, and a madly puffing engine dragged us over the wind-blown sands up through the hills of Judea to the little modern station just without the walls of Jerusalem. Once when we stopped at old Lydda we heard a rushing, whirring sound over our heads. It grew louder and, as we searched the sky, a

plane swept out from the soft clouds into the
clear blue, came down nearer, nearer to earth,
rose again, and passed out of sight. It had
come from the City of Zion: it would go into
Egypt.

The Wilderness, the Dead Sea and the forty
long years of wandering, the victories over the
Philistines, the waters of Jordan parted for the
passing of the hosts of Jehovah, the tumbling
walls of Jericho, the spots where "the arm of
the Lord prevailed": with these we had long
been familiar. They were associated in our
minds with tents, with much cattle, with slow
beasts of burden, with men, women, and children who moved leisurely in times of peace and
fled in wild confusion in times of war.

The Wilderness, the Dead Sea, the Jordan,
and Jericho we saw. A motor car driven by the
son of an Arab chief took us over and past them
all in less than a day!

Old Palestine still lies between the great
desert and the seas. The women still grind
the corn, stand gossiping about the well, and
wrap their babies in swaddling clothes. The
shepherds wander through the bare hills with
their sheep and lead them, when spring comes,

to the green pastures and the still waters. But there are *New Paths Through Old Palestine.* They cross age-worn desert-ways, go down into the shadows of deep valleys, climb hoary mountains, follow Elijah's chariot through great spaces of the sky. The new paths bring new days fraught with possibilities. In time they *may* bring a new Palestine: not the mystic land of the Zionists but the promised land of which the prophets and poets of Israel sang. Old Palestine died in nineteen-fourteen with the rest of the world that was and will never be again. New Palestine is born. What its future shall be depends upon the souls of those who follow the new paths. They may lead only to temporary triumph, to the selfish goals of the kingdoms of men: they *may* lead to the Kingdom of God.

Morgaret Slattery.

NOVEMBER 1, 1921.

ix

"Ah no! that sacred land
Where fell the wearied feet of the lone Christ
Robs not the soul of faith."
     —Richard Watson Gilder.

CONTENTS

I GO UP TO JERUSALEM

Our feet are standing
Within thy gates, O Jerusalem,
Jerusalem, that art builded
As a city that is compact together.—
Pray for the peace of Jerusalem.
Peace be within thy walls,
And prosperity within thy palaces.

Praise Jehovah, O Jerusalem;
Praise thy God, O Zion,
For he hath strengthened the bars of thy gates;
He hath blessed thy children within thee.
He maketh peace in thy borders.
                              —Psalms 122, 147.

I GO UP TO JERUSALEM

THERE was a moon that night. Now it was half hidden by soft clouds, now clear, brilliant, white against a velvet sky. We stood crowded close to the heavy ropes stretched across the bridge, which had swung open to permit one boat after another to pass. We were at Kantara on the Suez. Across the canal was the train dimly lighted, standing on the tracks that seemed half buried in the soft, yellow, desert sand. We waited impatiently. Nearly three hours had passed since the train from Port Said had left us there to attend to baggage and troublesome passports, and to eat a meager supper from boxes brought with us from the Port.

Now a Japanese boat passed slowly along the canal; then a smaller craft with cargo, flying the Dutch flag; a British boat brilliantly lighted, its passengers, many of them in uniform, dancing on deck. The canal is so narrow that great ships must creep slowly and carefully along, with no place for miles where one boat may pass another. It is a miracle, this

Suez Canal, and the story of its building a most
fascinating tale. Its banks are scarred by the
battles of the great war. Barbed wire, old dug-
outs, the remains of hastily constructed forts
reminded us of the desperate struggle made by
the Allies to protect it against the enemy in the
air and under the water. Had any one of their
many attempts successfully closed the canal,
the war would have had a very different ending.

We had just spent nineteen and one-half
hours coming through the canal at the slow
speed permitted by law—five miles an hour.
Even then our boat twice grazed the retaining
wall. In a single year over three thousand
boats passed through the locks, crept along
through the canal, then hurried to far ports,
east or west.

As the fifth boat swung lazily past, a sigh of
relief went up from the crowd pressed against
the ropes. A moment and the great bridge
moved back into place and we were given the
signal to cross. It was a weird group that
hurried along in the moonlight—a party of
Americans, a group of British officers, some
Australian soldiers, Jews from Russia clutch-
ing their permits to enter the land of promise,

4

Egyptians, Syrians, Arabs in native dress.
There were but few women. Our porter found
us seats close to the window in one of the compartments. We were sorry for this later, as
the fine sand sifted in and covered clothing and
baggage. No sleeping-car was possible, so we
made ourselves as comfortable as we could with
bags for pillows and heavy coats for blankets.
We were most grateful for this railroad from
Kantara to Jerusalem, realizing that before
the war we would have been compelled to make
the inconvenient and dangerous landing in the
small boats at Jaffa.

We made our way slowly through the night
across the desert that stretched as far as the eye
could reach in the moonlight and slipped away
into blackness when the moon had set. What
it had cost the men who had laid those ties in
that wilderness of sand, under the scorching
rays of a pitiless sun, no history of war can
adequately relate. How often in those days, as
we looked reverently at old battlegrounds, we
searched for words with which to describe the
miracles performed by the engineering corps
of the fighting armies!

With the morning light, we began to see signs

5

of life on the desert. Great masses of cacti, in
clumps as tall as trees, with stems as thick as a
man's body, were growing but a few feet from
our windows. Here, during the war, the enemy
had hidden their machine guns, a refuge from
which they might safely do their deadly work,
practically certain that they could not be captured. Many a brave soldier of the Allies gave
up his life in agony, caught in the cactus hedge
to which the rush of battle had driven him, and
many an heroic rescue of a comrade held by
the cruel thorns took place on that desert plain.
When the cactus growth cleared and the desert
was unbroken we stared in amazement at what
seemed to be a line of dark earth—a road
made in the shifting sand. When we got nearer
we found it to be strips of chicken wire. This
wire was the solution of a problem that at first
threatened to tie up all the plans of Headquarters, for the heavy artillery and the loaded
motor lorries, sinking deep into the sand, made
progress impossible. The wire road was the
result of the ingenuity of some of the men in
the ranks. As the fine and coarse net used
alternately pressed down upon the sand it gave
the resistance that enabled the great guns and

6

loads of supplies to pass over places otherwise uncrossable. When they had passed, soldiers rolled up the wire, loaded it on the camels to be used again over some hard stretch ahead. The war over, it lay there rusting in the sand.

Again and again, as one crossed the battle-fields of Palestine, he saw evidences of the triumph of man's mind over earth's obstacles. Nothing was too ordinary, too commonplace, too insignificant to be used to further the success of the great cause. For fresh supplies of food and water, for "heavies" with which to batter down the defenses of the enemy, the army was for a time dependent upon temporary tracks of chicken wire laid in a waste of moving sand!

Against the horizon we could see the slow moving train of camels. A group of Arabs on horseback halted to watch us pass. We were in Palestine, that land of small distances and great deeds.

"I cannot believe that I am in Palestine," said the young daughter of a British officer who was to see her father for the first time in four years. "I have not been able to think of it as a real land. I know, in a way, that Moses and

Joshua fought here. But think of father's fighting here, too!" The girl had expressed the thought of hundreds of others who have studied the Bible stories, become familiar with the difficult names, drawn maps and located the cities of Moses and of Paul, marked the journeyings of Christ, but to whom the land has never been a real land and its records, shrouded in vague mystery, have never seemed a part of the earth. But now we knew it to be real. We began to comprehend "the wilderness and the solitary place."

It is only about the size of my own state of Massachusetts, I told myself again and again. Its greatest length is but one hundred eighty miles and it is nowhere more than fifty-five miles wide. If I had the railways and engines of home I could cross it in less than two hours. I could travel its entire length easily in five or six. But the present train, with its light engine, on a roadbed hastily made, parts of it finished under fire from enemy guns, moves slowly. We are stopping at Gaza.

Once Gaza was the largest city of the old country of the Philistines. I can almost see Samson, strong and powerful, coming down

8

over the hill called today Samson's Ridge, bearing the great city gates upon his shoulders while men stood aghast. I can see him too, blinded and powerless, walking the treadmill of his enemies. As I look out over the desert road, I remember the Ethiopian struggling to find the meaning of the words of the prophet Isaiah and young Philip running by his chariot, eagerly responding to the invitation to sit with him and explain the prophecy. Riding along through the dust, I can hear him talking with the ruler about Jesus and what He had taught of God and man; and, half-astonished at the quick response, I can hear the Ethiopian, as they came near to a place with water, saying, "Behold, here is water, what doth hinder me to be baptized?" But I am brought back suddenly from the long past. Men in British uniform are on the platform of the little station. They follow the mail bag eagerly, joking each other in clear English accents about the probable contents.

For eight months in nineteen hundred and seventeen, Gaza became again the center of a great battle area. We could see the remains of the Turkish trenches, dug deep into the earth and protected by great masses of wire

9

or by sand bags made from the gay colored hangings and curtains taken from the houses of its people. But in spite of all their careful preparations and their gallant defence, Gaza fell into the hands of the British troops whose splendid officers and men had braved heat, terrible thirst, sand-storms, deadly fire that robbed them of hundreds of their comrades, that they might take this important post on the road that was to lead them through untold suffering up to Jerusalem, as it had led other armies of days long ago. The British Tommies read their Bibles in their spare time these days. They read over again the battles of Israelites and Philistines which they had found very stupid when they were boys in Sunday schools but which are exceedingly interesting to them now. As they fought, step by step, for possession of that same land, they asked themselves if, battling against a foe to whom the desert was home, on trackless wastes whose every spring and rock was known, they could ever win. Never for a moment did they hesitate in their answer, but many a brave young officer and many a hardy soldier of Australia or New Zealand must have had misgivings as he looked at the cactus hedge,

10

miles deep, or out over the still, barren, hopeless desert hills.

We left Gaza to climb slowly up to Lydda, now called Ludd, where we were obliged to change cars. On all sides were signs of the fighting of two years before, and now and then white crosses or Turkish graves reminded us of the terrible price youth has paid throughout the long centuries of history to make this land holy indeed.

As we climbed up into the hills, it began to rain, the air was fresh and cool, the vineyards here and there on the hillsides brought great relief after the glare of the sands through which we had been passing for so many hours. Our first glimpse of Jerusalem was in the soft mist through which the sun was attempting to shine. The walls looked high and forbidding, the whole city, from its point of vantage crowning the hilltops, seemed to look down upon us as though we were but very little things, little and unimportant, come to gaze, without half understanding what we should see, upon all man has dreamed and suffered in his reach for God and happiness.

A thrill of anticipation had passed up and

11

down the corridor of the train. Not a person
sat in his compartment. Corridor windows
were opened and eager faces crowded about
them. The face of the young girl who was to
see her father after the four years of separation
was flushed with excitement, but the face of her
mother was pale and there were tears in her
eyes. She had given her two sons—one in
France and one in Mesopotamia—to the world's
great effort to preserve its freedom. I shall
never forget the light in the eyes of two thin,
haggard, long-bearded Hebrews, looking out
from the windows, then turning to speak with
each other in Russian words that, though unin-
telligible to us, seemed to be on fire with passion.
Their gestures were expressive of emotion that
could not be restrained. Long before the train
stopped they were at the door.

The faces of young British officers on leave,
coming up for the first time to see the city for
whose delivery they had prepared the way down
on the dry parched plain, were keen with interest; no detail of the approach escaped them.
The residents accustomed to the journeyings
from the Port to the city looked at us all with
mild curiosity and kind tolerance.

12

I Go Up To Jerusalem

From the station, the horses dragged us up through gray mud that flew about us in showers, covering carriage, baggage, and robes,—there was no escape from it. From the mist the walls of the "city of cities" emerged, clear, strong, unbroken, no mark of battle upon them. As we went through the great gate, the sun, breaking through the mist, flooded with light, for a few moments, the narrow street and brightened the faces of the crowd of people of every nation that poured ceaselessly in and out. We stopped before the hotel that during the war had served as the Red Crescent Hospital. Lunch was waiting and we sat down with the Mohammedan in his red fez, the Bedouin in his long, beautiful, gay-colored coat, the French officer and the British officer on leave, Jewish business men, the Greek and the Syrian—the world, it seemed to us as we listened to the various languages. All orders for food were given in French, and in French men of different nations spoke with each other in courteous greeting.

At last the city of cities—Jerusalem. Here at the gate was David's tower; King Solomon once lived over there on the hill in his glittering palace and by his wealth and wisdom

made himself famous throughout the world,
and here he lost his wisdom as has many another
in the courts of the women. Herod and Pilate
looked out over these hills; the Crusader
stormed the walls and the Turk brought terror
and slavery with his sword. Twenty-three
times in its history Jerusalem has been captured. It has been pillaged, plundered, burned,
utterly destroyed, rebuilt only to be plundered
again. Yet here it stood. Upon what unspeakable sorrow the stars of Palestine have looked
down! We gazed from our balcony out over
the low buildings of solid rock, out through the
break in the wall made that the Kaiser, on his
visit to the Holy Place, might enter in great
pomp and glory with his impressive army of
followers, the break redeemed by the simplicity
of the entrance of the victorious General
Allenby into the city that he had conquered
without the destruction of a single building or
a foot of wall and accepted, when surrendered,
as a sacred trust placed once more in the hands
of Christians. It may be that the white crosses
in long rows, out on the hillside, guarding the
graves of soldiers from every part of the British Empire, young, very young, will continue

14

to remind these latest conquerors of the tremendous cost of the victory that left the city unharmed and help them govern the land with an unselfishness of purpose that will measure up to the high standard of their victory.

After lunch we found that dark clouds had gathered low over the hills, and before we could leave our room the rain came. We studied the map of the city, searched out the location of its sacred places, read over again the words of poet and prophet describing the days of its great glory, when from Mount Zion king and shepherd could look over at Mount Moriah where the smoke of the sacrifice from the temple of Jehovah ascended to heaven.

Late in the afternoon the rising wind scattered the clouds and the sun set in a blaze of glory. We stood just outside the gate on the city wall looking down across the valley over toward Bethlehem. The hills, deep purple, reached up on every side to touch the sky. Their bare rocky slopes became soft as velvet in the fading light.

A young British private, leaning against a part of the parapet, took out a khaki Testament and turned the leaves slowly. He seemed to find what he wanted and read, following the

15

lines with his finger. Then he closed the book, put it back in his pocket and turned, half apologetically to a companion not in uniform.

"We fought out there," he said, "the 53rd division. We fought around the very hills where the angels sang about Peace on earth."

A moment of silence and the other spoke: "Yonder is the road He must have climbed when He came up to Jerusalem."

"I'll take you over it tomorrow," was the answer. "We'll see all the places where He used to go. It makes the story in the Book very plain."

They moved away. Reluctantly, in the face of coming darkness, we left the great wall and joined the group of Arabs who, with camels and donkeys, were passing in and out of the gate. As we climbed the long stairs to our room, we remembered that tomorrow would be Sunday at home. In thousands of churches all over the world, trusting little children, strong, courageous youth, men and women bearing heavy burdens, the old, the sick, the missionaries would read the story of what He did and said centuries before, in and about Jerusalem—the story that, despite the limitations of those who have told it,

16

has changed the world and that must continue to change it until it shall become what He prayed it might be—the kingdom of God upon the earth. Tomorrow we, like the young soldier in khaki, would begin our journeys to "all the places where He used to go." And we hoped that for us, too, the sacred spots would "make the story in the Book very plain."

In a long procession with torches the worshipers of the Greek church, chanting an evensong for their feast day, passed beneath our balcony. A torch lighted up the cross held high over the heads of the marchers. Out over the hills of Bethlehem, hidden now by the night, bright stars were shining. We fell upon our knees and worshiped Him.

I GO OVER TO BETHLEHEM

There was a baby born in Bethlehem.
  I know they say
That this and that's in doubt, and, for the rest
That learned men who surely should know best
Explain how myths crept in, and followers'
      tales confused the truth.

I know—but anyway
There was a baby born in Bethlehem
Who lived and grew and loved and healed and
      taught
  And died—but not to me.
When Christmas comes I see Him still arise,
The gentle, the compassionate, the wise,
Wiping Earth's tears away, stilling her strife;
Calling, "My path is Peace; My way is Life!"

                    —Author Unknown.

I GO OVER TO BETHLEHEM

IT was clear and cold. The hills of Moab were deep blue. They seemed very near. In a low carriage that bore every mark of long service, drawn by two thin dark horses and driven by an Arab in a dull brown Bedouin coat, with the long, heavy head-dress falling over his shoulders and protecting him from rain or sun, we drove out through the gate. Dark eyes watched us curiously. The horses at first were swift of foot and the carriage lurched and rolled down the steep grade of the valley of Hinnom, past the former German colony, over the new bridge; then, losing their enthusiasm, they climbed slowly. On a hillside the sheep were feeding, but how they could find enough to sustain life on those bare rocky slopes is hard to understand. Now we passed a flock following the shepherd in his vari-colored coat down a steep incline and through a valley which in the rainy season would be a rushing stream. We could hear the lambs call, and now and then the shepherd's reprimand to a straying sheep.

Over there were the fields of Boaz. How beautiful they must have looked when the heavy sheaves of wheat were yellow in the sun. The land of Moab seemed such a short distance away as we who had been half-way round the world thought of distance, but to loyal, faithful, loving Ruth those desert plains, rounded hills, and deep valleys meant distance enough to separate her forever from the home and kindred she must leave behind. The brave words came back to us: "Whither thou goest, I will go; thy people shall be my people and thy God my God." She deserved the happiness she won out there in the fields as she followed the reapers. As if agreeing with our unspoken thoughts our guide turned and looked down at us. "Boaz, the owner of the field, married Ruth, the Moabite girl. She was very beautiful," he said.

The wind was bleak on the hilltop as it was that night centuries ago and we were glad when we reached the protection of the low stone houses of the village of Bethlehem. Such a tiny village! Nothing was left of the glory of that other day when the busy tax-gatherers checked up the names of the people and the keeper of the Inn hurried about trying in vain to find room for his guests, when officers of the army in resplendent uniform and civil officers proud and haughty made every Jewish pilgrim conscious of the power of great Rome.

Nothing remains of the old inn or khan which was crowded on that night to its very gates. Thankful indeed must both Joseph and Mary have been for the protection of the cave with its great manger hewn out of the rock. Over that spot to which they went so gratefully for shelter now stands the Church of the Nativity. It is a simple beautiful church, but the shrines within are garish indeed.

By General Allenby's command, the high forbidding walls of stone that have so long divided the interior and marred its beauty have been taken down. The walls had formerly separated the church into sections claimed by the various faiths. The nave of the church belongs to the Greeks, one transept to the Coptic Christians, the other to the Armenians. The Romanists have built a church and monastery close beside the little church of the Nativity, but worshipers could only reach the grotto to kneel at the manger of stone through a devious, difficult underground path. When the Turks captured

23

Palestine they compelled the Armenians to open a passage through their wall that the Romanists might enter. As we stepped into the church we heard the chanting of their choir, and soon through the door in the Armenian transept came priests and altar boys in the rich robes of the church to say mass. We stood aside until they had passed and only the echo of their voices could be heard floating up from the cave below.

Ever since the coming of the Turks, Christmas and Easter services have been marred by desperate quarreling and bloodshed. At each service Turkish soldiers were on guard and swords and guns punished offenders but were unable to prevent the paying of old scores by Armenian and Romanist, Copt and Greek. The British general was exceedingly anxious that no such quarrels should mar the celebration of the first Christmas and Easter after the return of the holy places into the hands of Christians, to be theirs no matter what their creeds might be. In many languages, he made his appeal to the people. The American Colony of Jerusalem was asked to be present at the services to help quiet any trouble-makers, but they did not wish to assume the responsibility. Therefore certain

24

individual members of the Red Cross Commission answered the General's appeal, and were present all day at the services, quietly warning any of the rougher element who, as in the past days, attempted to start trouble by taunting words. Not a British soldier was present. The Commission members, wise, alert, and friendly, did their work well and the day passed in dignified impressive worship for the first time since the Turks took the Holy City. The General expressed his gratitude in most cordial notes of thanks to the men who had so successfully endeavored to carry out his wishes.

We waited until the mass was over and then, with our lighted candles, went down into the shadowy grotto. Myth and legend, superstitions weird and fantastic have gathered about all the sacred places. While these things mean little to the modern Christian, he is bound to respect the reverent belief in them held by many of his comrades in the faith. With confidence the guide tells of the hundreds of years the fire in the hidden place has burned, not once going out, just as it has burned in the Church of the Holy Sepulchre at Jerusalem. If, as one kneels and prays, holding his taper close to the open-

25

ing, it is lighted by the unseen holy fire, rich
blessings will come to him and those he loves.

I shall never forget the thin, tired, sorrow-
marked face of an Armenian woman whose
taper, as she knelt murmuring prayers, suddenly caught the sacred flame. It was transformed. She went up the shadowy steps in
a transport of joy. Nor shall I soon forget
the face of a Russian woman as she swayed
back and forth on her knees in an agony of
prayer. When at last she rose she could not
stand and a kindly attendant steadied her.
He spoke to her in Russian and they talked
softly for a moment. She was in Jerusalem on
a pilgrimage when the war broke out. Her hus-
band, her son, and a son-in-law were in the Russian army. Of them she had had no word. She
had received a month since confirmation of the
news of the death of her two daughters in
prison. She could not go back to her home in
the hot-bed of Bolshevism. She took a taper
from the hand of a priest and went toward the
place of the holy fire.

I was glad when we were in the fresh crisp
air again, wandering through the streets of the
little village, stopping for a few moments for

26

"'Twas a humble birthplace, but oh, how much God gave to us that day!"

coffee with a Syrian shopkeeper who wanted to sell us olive-wood beads with a beautiful carved cross as pendant. His son, a boy of twelve, spoke English. The father brought him out proudly. He attended a Quaker school for boys over in Ramallah and was having a holiday. The souvenirs offered for our inspection were poor tawdry things, but the faces of the salesmen were so eager that we could not disappoint them. Visitors had been exceedingly rare during the years of the war and curious friendly eyes followed us hopefully everywhere. There had been great excitement in the village that morning. An Indian prince who was a Christian had visited the church, had left a gift for the priests, had made purchases in all the little shops—his taper had been lighted by the holy fire.

We were just about to go back to our carriage when, turning the corner abruptly, we were face to face with the young Britisher and his friend who had stood on the wall with us in the sunset the night before. He was pointing out over the hills. We smiled our recognition and asked if we too might hear of the coming of the army to Bethlehem.

"There is not much to tell," he said, in the

way of those who have risked all in battle. He told us a little about the difficulty of the fighting in the Judean Hills, the gigantic task of feeding the army and supplying it with water, the intense sufferings of the men in the cold drizzling rain and the chilling wind on the hills. Wrapping our own coats tightly about us, we could understand something of what they must have endured lying out on the bare unprotected hillsides as they did those nights before the city of Jerusalem was captured. After a moment he pointed out to us the hill Beit Jabor two miles northwest of Bethlehem won by the Welsh Division troops and opening the door for the entrance into Bethlehem, showed us the great house just south of Bethlehem where the Turks had seven mountain guns turned upon the road over which the troops must pass. But a thick heavy impenetrable fog settled down and, taking the risk, the heavy guns of the British passed up the road within easy reach of the enemy had they known. "Whenever a fog settled down like that, to our advantage, the boys would say, 'the Lord sent a great fog,' or 'the Lord hath covered the moon with a cloud'; but when rain or moonlight favored the enemy

28

they said nothing." He smiled. "The war is over," he said, "yet it seems as if at any moment this silence might be interrupted by the booming of a gun." "God forbid!" said our guide fervently. "We have had enough of guns." We echoed his words heartily as we said a warm word of appreciation of what British arms had done and went back to our carriage.

Two miles or more outside the village we looked down upon the place of Rachel's tomb. There have been few more beautiful stories of devoted service for love than that of Jacob who had "loved Rachel" and laid her there with a breaking heart. The simple, homely record of the joys and sorrows of every-day life written in the Book that is so full of human interest seems very real indeed as one looks into the faces of men and women about him, almost any one of whom might have played the part of hero or heroine without change of costume on a stage with scenery set. A little further down the long hill we stopped while the guide pointed to the place where the shepherds had watched their flocks. It was a plain lying close between the higher hills. Even on a chilly night it would be a sheltered spot and, huddled close together with the fire blazing near and the watchman at the gate of the fold, shepherds and sheep would be safe and warm. So they lay that night when the dark sky was suddenly flooded with light and voices sang over the awestruck hills of Judea.

We looked back at the little spot on the hill that was Bethlehem, where that night was born the baby who turned the world upside down— the baby who inspired the world's best art, its finest literature, its greatest music,—there in that little town with its stone houses, its irregular streets, its simple people struggling with poverty! There was Bethlehem, the city of David, the shepherd boy of the hills, strongest and best of all the sons of Jesse, born to be a king and through his long line of descendants at last to give to the world the King of kings.

When we stopped at the desk for our keys and to ask for a fire in the little square stove in our room the clerk, in hesitating, careful English, said, "You have found it cold out on the hills. You have seen Bethlehem. It is a small place, Bethlehem. There is little there that a man may do. Many travelers are disappointed by Bethlehem."

30

I Go Over To Bethlehem

"That depends upon how much one sees when he looks at Bethlehem," I thought. For me it held no disappointment.

That night in the great hall, around the stove that could not warm it, men talked of the future of Palestine. A good friend, who understood many languages and spoke Arabic fluently, interpreted much of the talk for us. The present population of Palestine, Jews, Christians and Mohammedans, is not even a million! Jews and Christians together number perhaps less than one-third. The Mohammedans make up most of the population and are found in every city and village. Arabic is the language of the people, but in Jerusalem and in Jaffa most European languages are freely spoken. The people who live in the towns are called Madani-yeh, the villagers are the Fellaheen, and those who live in tents, whom we called Bedouin, are Arabs. Despite its rocky, unpromising hillsides and its deserts, Palestine is an agricultural country and that must be its future, the men told each other. Wheat and barley, maize and lentils, figs, watermelons, grapes, pomegranates, mulberries, apricots, tomatoes, oranges, and olives could be easily raised. We heard

31

glowing descriptions of the Jaffa oranges and some sent later to our room fulfilled all that had been said of them. There was much talk of the day when the cultivation of raisins and the manufacture of olive oil would make men rich; talk of the bananas that could be made to grow in large quantities at Jericho and of the date palms that would make Gaza prosper once more. There must be new plows, new machinery of many sorts. They talked of the Zionist movement, but the talk was cut short by an Arab who would not hear of it and, as some faces darkened and voices grew louder, our friend rose and took us to our room. Sometimes in these days a friendly talk about Palestine's future ends in hot words and even blows. The Arab does not want Palestine to be passed over into the hands of the Jews. Many of the Jerusalem Jews express no pleasure whatever over an influx of their brothers from many lands. The problems of Palestine today are very grave and only great wisdom, unselfishness and patience will solve them.

After trying in vain to warm ourselves over our small wood stove we put on our heavy coats and stepped out upon our little balcony. There

32

was no moon. Save for a light over the Jaffa gate and soft rays from the windows of our hotel, Jerusalem was dark. The narrow little street at our left was black. The stars were clear, sparkling, very near. One star seemed larger and brighter than all the rest. As if unconscious of my presence my friend sang softly:

> " O little town of Bethlehem,
> How still we see thee lie!
> Above thy deep and dreamless sleep
> The silent stars go by.
> Yet in thy dark streets shineth,
> The everlasting Light;
> The hopes and fears of all the years
> Are met in thee tonight."

We hurried to our beds with their gay colored hangings and lay buried under blankets and rugs for warmth. For a long time, gazing out into the darkness, I could see the star.

O little town of Bethlehem! Small indeed— but spreading over all the earth. Only a few days before in America millions of children had heard its story, hugged their precious gifts, and thought of the angels and the shepherds. Thousands of parents, forgetting the pressure of dull gray days, filled with problems of food, clothing and shelter had smiled upon their own

33

children and thought tenderly of the Child, and
many men and women without a child to love
remembered the days of their own childhood
and greeted each other with "Merry Christmas." Small indeed—but I had heard the children of Japan with beaming faces sing its story;
I had heard the youth of China with strong,
beautifully serious faces tell of white gifts to
be given in the name of the Child who found His
way into the world out there on the hilltop of
Judea; in India I had heard the story told by a
girl whose face shone in the telling, as rows and
rows of little dark faces looked up at her. I
knew that in the sands of African deserts, in
the snows of Arctic lands, in the farthermost
islands of the sea, they had heard of Bethlehem.
A long line of familiar words surged through
my mind—democracy, freedom, liberty, justice
for all, the brotherhood of man, love—as women
may say it in Christian lands: . . . how many
of them were also born with Him that night in
Bethlehem!

No, "thou Bethlehem in the land of Judah
art not the least among the princes of Judah,
for out of thee shall come a ruler . . . and his
name shall be called Wonderful, Counsellor,

Mighty God, Everlasting Father, Prince of Peace.''

The wounded, hungry, puzzled world—the memory of the sufferings I had looked upon pressed hard upon me. I closed my eyes to pray that men may have the courage so to love and the faith so to act that the Prince may soon come into the possession of His kingdom.

When I opened my eyes, low over the hills against the blackness of the sky the star was still shining.

I GO DOWN TO JERICHO

"He passed by on the other side."

That 'other side' is trodden smooth
And worn by footsteps passing all the day;
Where lie the bruised ones faint and torn
Is seldom more than an untrodden way.
Our selfish hearts are for our feet the guide,
They lead us by upon the other side.

—Author Unknown.

I GO DOWN TO JERICHO

AN interested group surrounded us that morning at nine o'clock as the car which was to take us down to the Dead Sea and the Jordan drew up to the door of the hotel. I call it a car by courtesy. It had seen hard service. It had a battered running board, a mudguard with many dents, a front seat bending in the middle to the breaking point, no windshield and no horn. We protested, but our guide said it was the best that could be had.

"It is the engine that is important," he said, "the engine and the brake both are good. As for the horn, no fear—he is a horn with his mouth." He was a most successful human horn as we found when we passed through the gate into the traffic outside the wall. Our guide was not an enthusiast on the subject of motor vehicles. As we swept around the hairpin curves he was restless. "The Arab is not the temperament for a driver of cars," he said seriously, "he is the temperament for a horse." And again after a pause, "It is well to go to Jericho in a carriage.

39

The inn near Elijah's Spring is a good place for a rest, and three days—it is a good time for the trip.''

There was little traffic passing after we turned onto the long hill—donkeys with panniers loaded with products to be exchanged in the markets of Jerusalem, a boy driving a few sheep slowly up the steep hill, a lone Arab on his horse. The air was still, crisp, and very clear. We were exceedingly thankful for the road built by the Turks in excellent fashion for the visit of the Kaiser twenty-three years before and carefully repaired by the British troops for military service. We passed the rest house built that William Hohenzollern might refresh himself before approaching the Holy City. Lower and lower into the valley we went. The road now had a thin covering of soft gray mud. Suddenly, turning to avoid a huge rock that had rolled down the hillside into the road, the car skidded. A second and the light machine had crashed into the retaining wall of rock and cement. The axle bent, the front wheels turned at an angle, we were thrown back and forth in our shaky seat. The car stopped. We heard the sickening thud of the rocks as they fell to the dry bed of the stream below. Then we climbed down carefully over the loosened mass of cement. "Thank God we are to live!" said the guide reverently. The driver was trying to turn the wheels back. He pushed the car into the road. The engine would still run but the axle looked hopeless. The guide spoke again—"As I have said, a carriage is better for Jericho." After all our effort, we had failed to impress him with the fact that for us to give three days to the trip was impossible. "Of old," he continued, "they fell here among the thieves. We have fallen among the rocks." We could not help smiling at his look of dismay as he walked around the car again and again. He was so proud of his record of over thirty years as guide to whose care was due the fact that no serious mishaps had ever befallen any of his people. We were so grateful that we were not lying down there among the jagged rocks in the dry bed of the stream that our present difficulty seemed slight indeed. We were midway between Jerusalem and Jericho. If no help came we could walk in either direction twelve and a half miles though the prospect was not tempting. While we were discussing it we heard a

41

rumbling, then a horn. It was a British hospital car taking an officer down to Jericho. It was pay day for the soldiers and he was late. The driver of his car felt sure that with a little help the axle might be repaired enough to enable our driver to crawl back to Jerusalem, but the steering gear had been damaged and it would be an uncertain venture. A lorrie was on its way to Jerusalem and was to wait at the Good Samaritan Inn to give a message to the officer. He would leave instructions for them to help our driver back to the city and he could get aid for us. The men in the lorrie which came along according to schedule looked the car over with the air of expert mechanics. They spent a half hour or more on it with the help of our driver and then the little Ford turned and climbed slowly and bravely up the hill, keeping with greatest difficulty close to the safe side of the road. The lorrie was out of sight in a few moments flying along to make up for lost time. It would take word of our trouble and send another car.

There was nothing to do but wait and nothing to see but bare hills. We climbed one great rocky mound only to see more hills with deeper

42

There lay the boat in which one might row across the Jordan to the land of Moab.

valleys lying between as far as the eye could reach. They reminded us of the hills in the most desolate part of the Mormon trail in our own American desert. The sun rose higher and the heat became almost unbearable. We drew down our hats, put on our dark glasses and sat on the rocks in the dry bed of the stream. There was not a sound, not a bird note, no bleating of sheep. There were caves in the side of the hill. They looked dark, cool, and inviting, they had sheltered many people good and bad during the long centuries, but the guide warned us that they were full of vermin and unclean. There was a tiny boulder half-way up the hill which made on one side a narrow strip of shade and we made ourselves as small as possible and sat there.

Noon came and we ate our chicken and hard boiled eggs, French bread, figs, dates and oranges made ready by the hotel, and drank the water in our thermos bottles sparingly. A group of Arabs clattered past us over on the road. One sang a couplet in a clear, ringing voice and the others joined as in a chorus. They did not see us, or, if they did, made no sign. "When the Turks ruled Palestine," said our guide, "we could not sit here so safe. There

was much danger on this road and no man
traveled over it at nightfall.'' He told us tales
of brigands in league with Turkish high officials
with whom they shared their spoil that would
have made excellent material for certain types
of American motion pictures. Suddenly the
simple story that Jesus told to the crowd in
answer to the half-mocking question of the keen
Jewish lawyer came vividly before us. It was
in these hills, in the desperate loneliness of
them, that the certain man, stripped of all his
goods, beaten and half dead, lay helpless. He
might wait for help for many an hour before out
of this place of emptiness any would come! How
could Priest and Levite pass him by on the other
side and leave him in this forsaken spot that their
own journey might be undisturbed? To them
he was only a man robbed by the bandits. He
would die as had many another. It was a common thing, and, inhuman as it seems, they went
on to their task of holy worship and to the seat
of judgment.

How keen was the mind of Christ! How
quickly and unerringly He put his finger upon
the very center of sin! It was easy to see, coming down the narrow camel path in the hills,

44

the hated Samaritan with the spirit of justice, mercy, and brotherhood in his soul. He stopped —the man one would least expect to stop—and rescued with generous tenderness the suffering victim of thieves, while the servants of Jehovah and his law passed by on the other side, doing in that day even as, in all the days since, the followers of the letter and not of the spirit of the law have done.

There was only one answer to the question the lawyer had asked of Jesus and he was forced to give it—"He that showed mercy." I doubt if any who had heard the question, "But who is my neighbor?" ever forgot the answer, or the command that followed it: "Go and do thou likewise."

I was so lost in a new sense of the significance and sincerity of His wonderful teaching that I did not see our guide make his way toward the road. "A car comes," he called, but we, lacking his desert-trained senses, heard nothing. Two or three minutes and we could see it coming rapidly along the white road on the farther hillside. The guide was overjoyed when he saw the new driver. "Ah!" he said, "this is the man I wanted. He drives anything that

45

can go. Through the war he drove over hills with no road—always safe! He speaks English, too." He examined the car. It had both windshield and horn. It had an extra tire and seats that were straight. Hope revived.

"We shall now get quickly back to Jerusalem," said the guide. "Tomorrow, perhaps, we shall have the carriage." "To Jerusalem!" we said. "It is only one o'clock. With such a driver we can surely get to the Dead Sea and the Jordan. If it is late we can stay tonight at the Inn near Elijah's Spring and go back to Jerusalem in the morning. Our time is short and we cannot take another whole day." Jamil looked at the driver. "They are Americans," he said, "and when they will go, they will go!" After a moment he added, "The sun has been very hot. Perhaps for you it has dried the roads."

So we climbed the steep grade, ran along a level strip, then a steeper grade to the Inn of the Good Samaritan where Arab traders and men of the caravans stop for coffee. There was a tank in the yard where one could buy gasoline!

The road before us was down grade now, and the driver more than lived up to his reputation.

46

Once Jamil turned to show us a Mohammedan mosque in ruins in a desolate spot high up in the hills and again to point out a tomb. "It is the tomb of Moses by the word of the Mohammedans," he said; "but we do not believe it, for no man knoweth where God hath buried him. He never came into the land so we shall not believe it."

Neither of us who took it will ever forget that ride through the Wilderness. There was no road. Two deep ruts here and there marked our way. We wound through soft ooze turning now into the rut, now out again. On every side were hillocks of soft gray sand. "This is a good place to ride the donkey's back," said Jamil as we bounced up and down in the car, but he smiled. We told him we had motored to Germany over the shell-torn roads fording the bridgeless streams and this seemed very simple. Three miles of it and we were on a rough road close by the Dead Sea.

It lay still and calm, a blue gray thing crossed here and there by ribbons of silver where the sun glistened upon it. I should have said it had no motion but for the tiny little ripples that broke on the pebbly beach made frosty with salt

47

deposit. A thousand feet and more below the Mediterranean it lay there. Sitting beside it we were lower than any submarine has ever been. The city of Jerusalem is two thousand five hundred feet above the level of the sea so our descent had been over thirty-five hundred feet since morning. It was very warm. Though the great body of water lay there now so still, Jamil told us that when the Turks were using it to transport supplies, fierce storms swept over it, thunder roared in the hills and over the plains, and giant waves dashed upon the smooth shore. We looked across the fourteen miles of sea to the plateau in the hills of Moab and knew that there was no living thing in it nor on its whole great stretch of fifty miles! Hungrily it swallows up the rivers and the tiny streams, the Jordan alone pouring millions of gallons into it every day, but never, never does it send out even a tiny streamlet. It grants no answer to the plea of the thirsty land that seems to reach down into it hopefully. We put our hands into the water four times as heavy as the Atlantic and they were covered with an oily salty deposit that would not come off until we had scrubbed with hot water. Suddenly we heard a

48

sound—the bleating of a sheep. It was so welcome in that dead silence! Beyond the bend in the shoreline was a tiny house with children and the sheep!

We walked slowly along over the smooth gaily colored little pebbles to the spot, half a mile beyond, where the car was waiting. But we turned to look back again and again. The great silent sea held for us the awful fascination of *death.*

There was a road of a sort across the plain to the Jordan. When the river is in flood this plain is covered inches deep with ooze, rank vegetable growths spring up, the brown bushes are green, clouds of mosquitoes, scorpions, vipers and all manner of crawling things make their home here for a season; but now there were only long cracks that crossed and recrossed in the dried mud. Twice our wheels spun round in pockets of soft gray clay, but small thick boards, a spade and dry sand helped us out. A turn and we could see the river!

To one who has never studied the geography of Palestine or to whom books of travel are strangers, that first sight of the Jordan must bring far greater disappointment than to one in

49

a way prepared for the dark, muddy stream whose swift current hurries on ceaselessly, gathering silt as it goes. Within its normal banks it is such a narrow stream! We stopped for a moment in the house where sweet Turkish coffee and oranges were served us and where the boats used by fishermen and by tourists who like to row across to touch the land of Moab lay moored to a tiny wharf. The banks were steep here and soft willows bent over them. We sat down in the little boat that swung lazily at its moorings. It seemed the strangest and the most wonderful of rivers, this little muddy stream! Over it the great hosts of Israel passed; along its banks John, coming out of the desert, preached the kingdom of heaven to the multitude; and here came even Jesus Himself to be baptized in the waters His presence made sacred. We dipped our bottles carefully into the stream and filled them with water as all pilgrims do. We listened to the stories of the feast days when pilgrims come down to the river to worship there; we read the story of Naaman and understood why the proud leper of the king's court, even at the command of the stern prophet, hesitated to bathe in its waters. We lived in another day. Proud armies marched over the plain toward Jericho and we could almost hear Joshua's ringing commands. We were brought back to our own day suddenly by the sound of a voice, a very American voice, singing in the distance, "Roll, Jordan, Roll." We looked at each other in amazement. After a moment's silence the voice rang out again, nearer now:

"Some day I'm going to murder the bugler!
Some day you're going to find him dead!
I'll amputate his reveille
And stamp upon it heavily,
And spend the rest of my life in bed."

We climbed out of the boat and up the bank. A man in the early thirties stood there with a sapling, root and all, in his hand. He was an American working with the British under a commission for reforestation. He was most enthusiastic over his work and painted for us a wonderful picture of the hills, now bare and desolate, and the banks of the river, with the low scrubby growth, transformed some future day into valuable fruit and olive orchards, irrigated pastures, great stretches of light timberland. Jamil shook his head. "There is much talk these days about the changes that are com-

51

ing to this land, but we shall see—we shall see and *then* we shall believe," he said. Our friend went into the little house for food and rest and we stood in silence watching the stream which artists for centuries have painted, the river which has always stood for separation, under whose spell poets have written their sad hymns —watched it rushing on pouring more and more water into the Sea that is *Dead*.

The dunes, yellow and gray, between which we rode on to Jericho were round as though a giant hand had played with them, smoothed them over, and left them there. Twice we passed low stone houses with cisterns of water cut in deep rock hidden below the surface, and there were oranges and green things in the garden in the midst of the desert. It was cooler and the air was soft and balmy. The walls of Jericho—City of Palms—though now there are none, had indeed fallen, but there was no fear upon the faces of the people. The once mighty city is now but an ordinary village of lower class Arabs, with a supply station, a few shops, and the hotel where British officers live. Traces of recent battle over the very ground where the men of Joshua had routed the ancient enemy

were all about us. The story of the taking of
Jericho from the Turks by British troops when
the river at its flood had to be bridged by boats
and the temperature ran to 120° and more, is as
thrilling, as fascinating, and as triumphant as
that of Joshua himself.

Passing through the center of the town, we
came to the orange groves. The air was fragrant with the perfume of thousands of jonquils
growing wild along the edges of the irrigated
section. The children offered two huge bunches
for sale and we rejoiced in them. Our driver
took twenty bunches for a friend to sell in Jerusalem. He tucked them away neatly in the
folded top of the car. We bought delicious
oranges and our machine became a chariot of
delight. We went out to Elijah's Spring, whose
waters, made sweet and wholesome by the
prophet, were responsible for the luxuriant
flowers and delicious fruit, past the home of
Rahab who had saved the spies in Joshua's day,
stopping for a moment at the spot where the
sycamore tree had sheltered the rich publican
Zacchæus when he determined to see Jesus. It
was easy to imagine the consternation that
filled the city when it became known that Jesus

53

had commanded him to come down because He
would be a guest in his house that day—the
house of a *publican*. It was on this road, too,
that Bartimæus met Jesus and, despite the demand of the multitude that he be quiet, continued to cry aloud until the Healer saw him,
opened his eyes and set his soul on fire with
gratitude. How close the multitude must have
pressed in those narrow streets, as driven by
curiosity and longing for help, they followed
Him! How often the body and soul of the Master must have cried out for the shelter of the
mountain, the stillness of that waiting desert
where in the night God could come very near
with a new message and new strength for the
coming day! It was at times like these, when
half carelessly they pointed out to us the spots
where on common days Jesus passed by, chang-
ing forever the lives that He touched, that we
loved Him.

The sun was creeping on toward the horizon.
We must turn back toward Jerusalem. Every
foot of the road the driver assured us he knew.
He would leave us in the Inn with the guide if
we wished and send for us early in the morning, but he would get back to Jerusalem. So

would we and he was content. He got all possible speed out of the car. It must climb back over those thirty-five hundred feet we had come down such a short time since.

We stopped a moment to peer at the lonely monastery where monks still live on the Mount of Temptation and pray daily for all who are tempted. The road which had been so lonely in the morning was stirring with life. Groups of Arabs on horses and little swift-footed donkeys moved aside to let us pass. Twice at a signal from a man riding ahead on horseback we stopped to let a great caravan pass us. The leading camels wore gorgeous trappings and tinkling bells. Once a camel without cargo, following in dignified fashion behind two others, stood perfectly still, trembled, then turned and ran ahead of us. We were amazed to see how swiftly he ran. In vain the rider of the other camel shouted and called. Had it not been for a friendly companion, who, coming down the hill, drove his own camel straight across the path, spoke soothingly to the great beast while a man on a donkey grasped his chain, he might have led us a chase all the way to Jerusalem. They did not attempt to take their prisoner past

55

us in the road but turned off into a deep defile. When we looked back from the hilltop they were again on the road moving on toward Jericho. But most of the camels bearing their burdens merely sniffed and passed us by in scorn.

It grew very cold as we reached the heights and the discarded robes and coats were welcome. We could see shepherds and sheep seeking places of shelter. Sometimes we caught glimpses of herds of goats reluctantly following or plunging ahead silhouetted against a soft violet sky. The sun set calmly and we missed the blazing glory. Suddenly it was night. We were glad to be well past the scene of our morning's mishap and nearing Jerusalem. When we stopped at the door of the hotel, Jamil gave a sigh of relief. "We have had a wonderful day," we said. "We have had a day of miracles," was his answer in a solemn, devout tone. Both he and the driver were most happy a moment later when they received their extra fee.

Dinner was over for most of the guests, but we were given a warm corner and more food than it would be possible to eat in many meals. We found that the entire hotel had joined in Jamil's sigh of relief when we returned. There was a snapping wood fire in the little stove and hot water bottles that made the great curtained beds seem more inviting. The maid wished us "sleep without dreaming."

But for a long time, lying there in the darkness, I dreamed with my eyes wide open. Dreamed of the forty years wandering in the wilderness while one generation passed and a new one was born. Dreamed of the kings and the prophets, of David hunted like a wild thing through the desolate hills and caves, of captives marching across the sands to Babylon. Dreamed of the Man who, with weary feet, in the heat and the dust *walked* about the Jordan Valley, through Jericho, walked up the long, long hills even to Jerusalem with men and women following, always *seeking*, only a few sharing. Dreamed of the demand that He made upon all who did have the courage to share—that they love God— and the challenge that they love their fellow men as He loved them, . . . dreamed of the day when the challenge would be answered and the other man's welfare would become each man's passion.

I GO TO BETHANY

I tell you when I looked upon these fields,
And stony valleys,—through the purple veil
Of twilight, or what time the Orient sun
Made shining jewels of the barren rocks,—
Something within me trembled; for I said:
This picture once was mirrored in His eyes;
This sky, that lake, those hills, this loveliness,
To Him familiar were; this is the way
To Bethany.

—Richard Watson Gilder.

I GO TO BETHANY

ONE afternoon when we were driving about the busy semi-modern streets that lie outside the walls of Jerusalem we suggested to Jamil, our guide, that some afternoon we walk to Bethany. He answered briefly that it was too far and turned to call our attention to the well-equipped postoffice, the modern looking shops, the Italian hospital, the well-built hospices of the French, Italians and Russians which before the war were thronged at the feasts with devout pilgrims. There was an atmosphere of western life about the outer city. Signs over some of the shops looked amazingly like New York's East Side. Books, pictures and maps, school supplies, men and boys' clothing of every sort, girls and women on the streets dressed in European fashion, together with Cairo papers in French and English, helped us to see the trend of the new, growing city without the walls. The streets were wide and well kept. The church of St. George was an artistic, beautiful reminder of the reason why the word of

the capture of the Holy City had been received
with solemn joy in every English household.
We passed the dignified Damascus Gate and the
Sheep Gate before which camels knelt grunting
and little groups of sheep huddled close each
around its shepherd; lorries passed us on the
road, then a motor taking General Storrs to
confer with the High Commissioner on important business. We stopped to visit the British
High School for girls, doing its work against
great odds in a former German orphanage
poorly equipped for school work. The girls of
twelve nationalities with most excellent *ésprit
de corps* were studying there; the principal, a
real educator, formerly head of the girls' school
at Beirut had wise, far-seeing plans for the
future of the school and, through it, for the welfare of the city. As I listened to them I wished
that my purse were well filled that I might make
some of them possible now in the day of crisis
when the whole future of Palestine is in the
making. Surely there are new paths through
old Palestine.

When we again entered the city through the
Jaffa Gate it seemed centuries older than when
we had left it, so great was the contrast between

the air, sunshine, and breathing spaces outside the walls and the narrow, dark, and crowded little cobble-stoned alleys, shared by man and beast, where no full ray of sun ever shines. Only the flat roofs of the houses save the people within the city from life in a semi-dungeon. It was this plunge back into the city of age-old days and deeds that made us long the more to walk leisurely to Bethany and so, on Saturday night, we told Jamil we should not need him until Monday morning at nine.

We left the city just after noon on Sunday by St. Stephen's Gate, stopping reverently for a few moments close by the steep hillside to think of the brave words of the young martyr as he looked into the hard faces of his accusers and his wonderful address, recalling to them each step of their history and the reason for each great defeat. We remembered the daring words: "Which of the prophets have not your fathers persecuted? and they have slain them which showed before of the coming of the Just One; of whom you have been now the betrayers and murderers: who have received the law by the disposition of angels, and have not kept it." In fierce anger they ground their teeth and

63

hissed their reproaches at him. But he did not even see them. Suddenly, looking up to heaven, they heard him saying, "Behold, I see the heavens opened and the Son of Man on the right hand of God." It was enough. Seizing him, they rushed him through the narrow street and cast him out of the city. They laid their garments at the feet of a keen young man named Saul, who watched with approval as they hurled down upon their helpless, suffering victim the jagged stones of the hillside. But above the noise of their mutterings of revenge the young man Saul heard the words of prayer: "Lord Jesus, receive my spirit." And again, "Lord, lay not their sin to their charge." And Stephen died—but Saul never forgot.

From St. Stephen's Gate the smooth, broad road makes a steep descent down to the valley of the brook Kedron, then it climbs again around the shoulder of Olivet, where we stopped to look back at the city with the dome of the mosque of Omar glistening in the sun. The air was clear and the hills, with the light, shifting clouds above them, changed color every moment. Jamil had told us that the hills about Jerusalem bore always "a luxuriant crop of stones" and

64

his words seemed true indeed, a crop made even more abundant by the heavy shell-fire of the months past. Still, in little square patches between the ridges, men were plowing. One plowman had a thin, patient ox and a donkey together under what seemed a heavy yoke. Here and there thick vines leaned against sunny walls as in the days when Jesus used them for the text of His great sermon "I—the vine: ye—the branches. Without me, ye can do nothing."

It was when we walked out a little from the main road to Bethany to look over into a deep valley that we saw a carpenter at work in his sunny yard, making yokes for the oxen. He worked deftly with his clumsy tools at his primitive bench. The court-yard was swept clean, save for the corner where the shavings fell. There were green things growing in a garden. After a moment a woman appeared in the doorway. She looked curiously at us but answered our smile. "Ing-leesh?" she queried. We shook our heads. "American," we said very distinctly. The man at the bench turned quickly. A shower of words in the Hebrew tongue and a motion to wait answered us. The woman hurried into the house and was back in

a moment with a photograph in her hand—a
man, a woman, two children. The photograph
was taken in *New York!* She pointed proudly
to the word. As we were about to leave, being
limited to conversation by means of nods, smiles
and gestures only, a boy came from the rear of
the house. He had great, dark, dreamy eyes,
his head was a mass of thick curls, in his hands
he had two irregular blocks of wood which he
gave to his father. He smiled at us shyly, but
turned to look again with frank interest and
curiosity when his mother repeated the word
American.

It was hard to tear ourselves away from this
picture of the carpenter with his little son and
the mother at the door, but there was no excuse
for lingering. We could only hope that this
young son of a carpenter might sometime know
the story of that other Son, of whose early days
in the village of Nazareth he served so forcibly
to remind us.

It is not a long walk to Bethany, a little over
four miles they told us, and we soon saw the low
gray stone houses with their roofs of mud not
far ahead. As we approached the village, a veri-
table host of children rushed to meet us, calling,

66

It was here that He came to talk with one who seemed to understand—
and there were so few.

with a score of accents, words supposed to be English. At first we covered our ears then motioned to one child to speak. We learned that they were offering their services as guides. The moment we appeared to understand, the babel began again. "Mary and Martha," they called. "Simon-Lazarus, I will show." When we spoke they listened, but only for a moment. "You cannot all be our guides," I said. "If you all follow we will go back to Jerusalem and no one will have *back-sheesh*—not one. We shall not look at the house of Mary and Martha." The tallest among them, a lad of fourteen, he told me afterward, evidently repeated our words and he emphasized them with a flourish of a stout cane which he carried. He showed us a soiled card with a name written upon it which he said was his. We chose him and one other guide, a little girl of six who had pointed to herself proudly, saying, "I know—I know, Mary —Martha—Lazarus." At a word from a villager passing on his donkey the children scattered and it was a great relief.

Our young guide knew the method perfectly. Driving the dogs out of the way with his cane, he led us up a steep path to the house of a man

67

who was a dwarf, badly crippled. He was to
take us to the tomb of Lazarus which he did,
when we had paid the piastres he asked. He
insisted upon telling us the story before we
went down the long winding stone steps worn
smooth by the passing of men's feet for centuries. He told it in very graphic fashion. We
had only the dripping candles to light our way.
Following him, we could hear his call at each
turn, "Have care! Have care!" We decided
not to make the entire descent of sixty steps but
contented ourselves with looking down from
the fortieth step into the black pit below. The
air and sunshine were most welcome when we
climbed back and, giving more piastres for the
shepherds' slings the old dwarf took from his
pocket, we left him happy. We stood for a few
moments at the entrance to the tomb, thinking
of all that spot had meant in the centuries since
it was recorded that, in warm human sympathy
with the suffering sisters, "Jesus wept."

We stood a long time on the wall of the ruins
that covered the spot where the home of the
three friends of Jesus had stood. It looked out
over the valley on one side and toward Jerusalem on the other. Our guides, big and little,

sat down on the stones and were silent. Nowhere in our journeys through Palestine did
we trouble our souls over the arguments of men
as to exact spots and identical places. If not
to the place of this ruined wall, then to some
spot near by Jesus came. Came to receive rest
for His body and comfort for His soul. Came
to forget for the moment Jerusalem with its
noise and confusion, its need and its hate.
Came to talk with one who seemed to understand
and sympathize—and there were so few. What
it would mean to us today if we could know the
many things about which Jesus talked that have
never been recorded for us! We remembered
that it was from Bethany over the hills through
which we had come that Jesus made his way to
Jerusalem on the day when He found the colt
and rode triumphantly through the streets to the
temple, amidst the shouted hosannas and waving palms that filled the Pharisees with jealous
anger. It was here that he may have spent the
nights of that last crowded week until the night
of the Supper when he sought the Garden. One
could feel, standing there looking toward Jerusalem, something of the agonizing sorrow that
swept over that household when they learned of

the trial that was a mockery of justice and the condemnation of their beloved friend to death on a cross.

When we were ready to leave, the young guide asked if we would like to go into one of the houses and see the upper room where a guest may sleep. We hesitated to walk in this fashion into a home but he explained that we were sure of a welcome and a little *back-sheesh* would pay.

The upper room was a clean and quiet spot. There were small woven rugs, a cot with hand-made covers spread over it. A bed roll stood in the corner. There was a heavy metal basin for washing and two lamps, ages old, filled with oil. The window was open toward the road that leads to Jericho. It was a place where one might rest his soul. "Many guests came to this room before the war," said the boy, "the family is large. Some live far away in Damascus. They come for the feasts. But not since the war— there is not money and some have died." The *back-sheesh* was accepted gratefully with many words of thanks by the two women below—one very young with a baby in her arms.

Our next stop was at the spot where once had stood the home of Simon the leper where a

70

woman did the Great Teacher high honor as she broke her very precious box of alabaster and, in an abandonment of love and gratitude, poured the fragrant perfume over His head. We could hear the petulant voices of those who complained because the ointment had not been sold for a good price and the money given to the poor. But Jesus understood.

"This is all for Bethany," said the guide of fourteen years. "It is not large and it is poor." We did not need his words to make us realize it. The little girl who had called herself *guide* so proudly had not spoken a word, but, as she had climbed over the steep places, had waited patiently, had listened intently to the boy, and had given us at every turn a smile which we remembered for many a day, she had earned her fee. When she received it she ran madly toward a house near by and disappeared. The boy walked with us courteously to the edge of the village. In response to our query as to where he had learned English he said, "Off a merchant I worked for since I was six. He lives just outside the city." The "off" with which he began his sentence sounded as though the merchant might at one time have lived in America.

71

At the outskirts of the village, where we had
met them as we entered, were the children.
They ran beside us shrieking *"back-sheesh"*
and holding out their very dirty little hands.
We shook our heads vehemently. It meant
nothing. Then we stopped and reminded
them that we had paid our two guides and
all the people who had helped us, but that
they had done nothing for us. "We are
poor," said a girl with a baby in her arms
as though that were reason enough for her
demand. I shall never forget the thin face,
the piercing black eyes of a boy, perhaps ten.
"America rich," he said, plendy, plendy,
plendy money." There was the deepest reproof
in his voice.

"Some people are *very* poor," I said, "the
children cry for bread. In the winter they are
very cold. There are many very poor people in
America."

"No," said the boy stoutly, and I saw that he
did not believe me, but he repeated what I had
said to the others. It was very hard to refrain
from giving them money, but we remembered
the request that we should not help to train a new
generation of beggars and steeled our hearts.

When we started on again a few accompanied us but we paid no attention and one by one they dropped out, having followed us almost a mile. Some said good-bye cheerfully, others made gestures of disgust. One lone lad still walked patiently beside us. He had great hollows under his eyes and, now that we could see him separated from the others, we noticed how very thin and pale he was, how ragged and dirty. In his arms he carried a baby whose eyes were in a pitiable condition, one so swollen that it was entirely closed. He said faintly in a weak, tired voice, *"back-sheesh—back-sheesh,"* over and over. He looked as though in dogged determination he would follow us back to the city gates. Unable to resist the pleading we yielded, gave him some coins, watched the light come into his eyes, saw him turn and make his way slowly back—one of these little ones who so easily perish while waiting for the coming of the kingdom of God—the kingdom that Jesus said was *theirs.* It may be that the school now being opened in the little village will help to bring them their rights.

When we told Jamil next day of the children he said, "Ah, that is why you should have me!

73

The guide saves you. You should not go alone, and walking you cannot get away."

"Where are the parents of these children," we asked.

"Poor," he said slowly, "very, very poor. Always poor and the war has made it very hard. It will be better now, but they have learned bad habits."

A turn in the road and the village was entirely out of sight. We overtook a flock of sheep and for a time walked slowly behind them. The bleating of the lambs who seemed weary sounded like the voices of the children. The shepherd turned into a narrow path between the hills, called in clear, urging cadences, and the sheep followed him. We climbed up from the road and sat on the rocks under gnarled old trees. A tower on the mount of Olives stood out clear against the sky. We read aloud of the Holy City from the words of the prophets and the Psalms of David.

Night would soon steal down over the valleys, so reluctantly we moved on past a cluster of tiny stone houses, past the cemetery of the Hebrews, when, flying up the hill at reckless speed, shaking us rudely back from the past into the

74

present, came a motor rushing toward Bethany. Bethany that seemed to be out of the world of motors! It was the doctor's car from the hospital, they told us when we described it. Just before the road drops abruptly into the valley we stopped to look again at the City. There was always something strangely gripping in the sight. The words of Jesus wrung from Him as, in deep compassion that was agony, He looked at the City, feeling the weight of its sin, its pain, its need, came back to us—"O, Jerusalem, Jerusalem, that killeth the prophets and stoneth them that are sent unto her! how often would I have gathered thy children together even as a hen gathereth her chickens under her wings, and ye would not!" We hurried on through St. Stephen's Gate.

On the hills it was light but in the narrow streets with their gateways and buttresses it was quite dark. We took out our faithful flashlights, and with our canes to help over the shadowed steps went rapidly up to the hotel that stood as a strong and sheltering friend in the faint glow that still lingered in the western sky.

"Not much in Bethany," they said to us at

the desk as they had said of Bethlehem. "Too far to walk for the few stone houses and the ruins."

How could they know what we saw in Bethany? How could they know the overwhelming sympathy that surged in upon us as we stood on the walls of "the house of Mary and Martha," looked upon the hills and valleys He saw in their purpling shadows, thought how much harder the friendship and fellowship of that home must have made it to remain true to the message that was to take Him to Jerusalem to die, thought of the short day of triumph, waving palms and lavish praise, thought of his youth and his glorious undaunted soul!

No, they did not know what we saw in Bethany.

76

I GO OUT TO THE MOUNT OF OLIVES

He turneth a wilderness into a pool of water,
  And a dry land into watersprings
And there he maketh the hungry to dwell,
That they may prepare a city for habitation,
And sow fields and plant vineyards.

Instead of the thorn shall come up the fig-tree; and instead of the briar shall come up the myrtle tree: and it shall be to Jehovah for a name, for an everlasting sign that shall not be cut off.

The latter glory of this place shall be greater than the former, and in this place will I give peace, saith Jehovah.

                                    —The Bible.

I GO OUT TO
THE MOUNT OF OLIVES

BEFORE we met our carriage at the Damascus Gate to ride out to the farthest point on the Mount of Olives we walked through David Street to the Wailing Place of the Jews. Every book we had studied warned us of the unspeakable condition of the narrow filthy streets in this Jewish quarter of Jerusalem the Golden. But they were all written before British arms had captured the Holy City and, even in these short months, made it in so many ways a new Jerusalem. In the windows of the shops we had seen the quaint pictures of the water-carrier with his leather bag, but not one had we seen in the streets of the city. The menace of the water bag with its myriad germs is already a thing of the past. For the first time in all its long history, under rulers of many great faiths and names, the City has water, plenty of water, fresh, clear, safe. What that simple statement means can be appreciated only by those who know by experi-

79

ence what a priceless boon water is to cities that have little. One could change the whole record and history of Oriental cities with water systems!

When the history of Palestine in the war is fully recorded, one of the most thrilling chapters will be written about the lead pipes now standing boldly in the city streets two feet above the ground, capped by very modern shining faucets. The girls and women who come to them with their water jars beamed with joy as they watched the silver stream pouring out in the sun. For four hundred years the Turks ruled in Jerusalem and in all that time no attempt was made to establish a water system although more than once the inhabitants were taxed with the promise of water that was some day to come. In a little over two months the British engineers had brought running water into every street of the city. New paths are so rapidly making their way through old Palestine!

For its water Jerusalem had depended upon winter rains to fill its great cisterns. The houses had underground reservoirs, some of which had not been cleaned in more than twenty years. At the Mosque of Omar was a large

80

reservoir where the water from the springs about Solomon's Pools flowed down through a great aqueduct built by the Romans when Herod ruled over the Jews. The searching engineers had found springs in the hills with fresh, pure water running to waste and, at the rate of fourteen thousand gallons an hour, it is now pumped up to the top of a high hill, run by gravity down through a long pipe-line to a great reservoir that has been built and carefully protected on the outskirts of the city. Direct lines take this pure water to the hospitals and into the city streets. Despite the shrinking of the population, caused by the evacuation of the Turk, more than ten times as much water has been used as in previous years, which silences the oft-repeated statement that the people would not appreciate the water if they had it. We were interested to learn that some of the pipes had been sent to Egypt to be forwarded for use in Palestine by the American Red Cross Commission after we entered the war. But the Commission found that the need for water which we had anticipated had been practically answered by the Royal Engineers.

One is deeply impressed by the change in the

record of contagious diseases. The reduction in cholera, smallpox, typhoid, and typhus is remarkable. Even under the sound of booming guns, children's welfare bureaus were organized, lessons in health given, nurses trained and kitchens opened to provide food for the babies, the sick and the old. The workers of the American Red Cross deserve and receive full gratitude for their enthusiastic and intelligent work in and about the City in those days immediately following its surrender.

The people on David Street seemed to have lost something of the fear that writers of the past saw in their haunted faces. It may be the fact that now they are free. The old-time pressure and petty persecution by corrupt officials is past. The Turkish prison no longer yawns threateningly. A trader may go unmolested about his work. The heavy taxation demanded in the past by a succession of officers, from the least to the greatest, has disappeared. Contentment not known for untold generations reigns in humble homes.

It may be for this reason that on both occasions of our visit to the Wailing Place there were but few present and they were old men,

From the brow of the Mount of Olives where they lay sleeping under white crosses—these also "fling to us the torch."

old women, and some very young children.
Young manhood was not there, it was hard at
work. Many of the older boys and girls were
in school. The leader of the group chanting
the Lamentations that morning was an old
white-haired patriarch with eyes of fire. He
was the only one of the group that did not inter-
rupt his wailing to look at us. One tall, strong,
impressive specimen of womanhood moved along
the line to quiet some women whose wailing had
become a piercing shriek or to straighten out a
child who irreverently chased a playmate up
and down the path. The guide said that her
name was Miriam and that she had a son with
much money in England. Erect and fine, force-
ful and devout, she reminded us of that other
Miriam who led her people to victory. Here
and there one saw women's strong faces stained
with tears and marked with suffering. They
leaned against the foundation stones of the old
Temple area in an abandonment of emotion and
sorrow. Near the end of the line was a very old
man leaning tremblingly upon his staff. Jamil
said that he was repeating one phrase over and
over. "O God, the heathen are come into thine
inheritance!" His voice was bitter and full of

anguish. A great wave of pity swept over us for these and all they have suffered, and yet survived. Against those massive walls of the past, Babylonian, Assyrian, and Egyptian had hurled their hosts and battered them to earth. They had risen again only to meet the Roman and the Saracen, the brave Crusader and the unspeakable Turk until in very truth they lay "in heaps." Piled one above another, the various cities lie waiting until the hammer and spade of the excavator shall open up all their secrets for us. Buried deep down in the earth is that early city of the Jebusites, over it the glorious city of Solomon, the city heroically brought again into being by Nehemiah, the city of Herod which Titus hammered into ruins and Hadrian rebuilt, above it the city of the Saracens built after their wave of conquest, the city of the Crusaders, and now the city of the Turks, standing boldly above the ruins of the long past. It stands, the protected property of a new conqueror who loves it, whose army chose the hardest road to victory to save it from the marks of war, whose people have come into it with knowledge that they may overcome its ignorance, a conqueror who bears no malice,

84

who is tolerant of the Jew and the Mohammedan though he worships at the Cross which they hate.

As if reading our thoughts, the guide said quietly, "Some day it will be only the wall for the wailing that we shall see. There will be no more need for wailing, and the children will forget. So the young prophets among the Jews say in the markets. We shall see."

We walked through a section of the Temple area and out past the Austrian Hospice through the Damascus Gate where, according to agreement, the carriage waited.

The road out to the spot where the Mount of Olives drops abruptly to the plain has been repaired, stray shell holes filled in and a large section of new road built since that wonderful day when the last line of Turks were driven from the position they thought secure. The air was as clear as an October day at home and the shining city "compact together" seemed substantial and strong. It was along the high ridge of Olivet that, in the pressure of the days when relief workers toiled twelve and fifteen hours without respite, they came to renew their strength. In the home of the Greek Patriarch more than one strong soul, overcome for the

85

moment by the ceaseless stream of dirty, hopeless, despairing human things that he must strive to save from the wreckage of war, found, in the white moonlight sifting down over the hill, in the kindly stars, in the silence and in sacred memories, courage to attempt again tasks that had been called impossible.

We had been gazing so steadily at the city that when the driver suddenly stopped we turned in surprise. There on a gently sloping stretch of ground, close to the road at the left, stood row after row of crosses over the resting places of Scot and Londoner, Welshman and Irishman, Indian and Anzac who had paid for the Holy City with his life. On some of the crosses fresh green garlands were hanging, and on one a wreath with English holly.

We got down from our carriage and walked slowly along, looking now at the crosses and now at the place where in agony of soul Christ had prayed for the strength to meet the test of Calvary that has made the Cross forever the symbol which shall mark the spots on earth most sacred to us. These lying out on the hillside had also been to Calvary.

A little farther on in the road we passed men

in the British uniform. They had survived the terrible test of those wind-swept hills with the rain falling in torrents, the benumbing cold, the soft, thick, gray mud, the night in the open with no shelter save a little wall of stones built up with care only to be blown over by a sudden vicious blast, with little food and only the ammunition that could reach them on the backs of the pack donkeys. It was through this they had won that peaceful city lying contentedly there in the sun, even the shining dome of its Mohammedan Mosque unharmed.

The German hospice, Kaiserin Augusta Victoria, lies out on this road. It is exceedingly well built and untouched by shell fire. Although the Turk utterly demolished the mosque of Nebi Samwill and shot away its stately minaret, he turned no gun on this that was German property. Even when his airmen, flying over Olivet, knew that an enemy signal station had been set up in the garden of the hospice no shot fell upon it. "This house," said Jamil, "is like a German castle on the inside. The tower was built higher than any tower on the Mount, the trees set out with care. The picture of the Saviour is painted in the chapel and the pictures

87

of the Kaiser and the Kaiserin are on the long
wall. It was common talk at the beginning of
the war that the Crown Prince should live here
when he became King in Palestine. Now it is
the Headquarters for the British Army. . . . It
is the Will of God!" he added solemnly after a
moment. We took a picture of the hospice with
two British Tommies standing at the gate.

We had to leave our carriage and walk to the
point where the Greek Church tower looks down
over the stretch of rugged upland crossed by
many a wadi, over the walled-in level spaces
where green things were growing, over the
plains of the Jordan and the Dead Sea so blue
in the distance, away to the far mountains of
Moab. It was a wonderful picture at which
one could look for long hours and come back to
enjoy again and again. It was from this point
of vantage that the relief workers watched the
taking of Jericho. In the grove we found the
"husks that swine did eat," lying about on the
ground. Jamil picked one of the long brown
pods from the tree and under the pressure of
his urging we tasted it. It was sweeter than
sugar cane, nauseatingly sweet. It took no
imagination to understand why one would

accept it as food only as a last resort. In this grove we found the hyssop which the women at the hospice use both as medicine and for the whitening of their clothes. In a sunny sheltered spot we found violets, although we were wearing our warmest wraps.

Jamil sat down on a stone to talk with a workman while we, wandering about on the slopes of the hill, found a warm sheltered spot looking toward Mount Moriah. In all the days that we were in Jerusalem we could not fully sense the fact that the Christian was now free to visit all the sacred places, that the Temple area was open to him, that he might enter the sacred Mosque of Omar which once it had been death to enter. *The Turk had gone!* We took out the Book and read the old instructions for the building of the Tabernacle, read the orders for the building of Solomon's temple and the majestic words of its dedication when at last the building was finished:—"and Solomon stood before the Altar and said—'O Jehovah, God of Israel, there is no God like thee in heaven above or on the earth beneath; who keepest covenants in loving kindness with thy servants that walk before thee with all their hearts. . . . But will God in

very deed dwell on the earth? behold the heaven
and the heaven of heavens cannot contain thee;
how much less this house that I have builded!
. . . When thy people Israel are smitten down
before the enemy because they have sinned
against thee; if they turn again to thee and con-
fess thy name and pray and make supplication
unto thee in this house then hear thou in heaven
and forgive thy people Israel and bring them
again unto the land which thou gavest to their
fathers." Of Solomon's Temple scarce a ves-
tige remains, yet Israel again is returning to the
land of its fathers. We read of the visits of
Jesus to the new temple which, great as it was,
had so little of the glory of the old. How it must
have thrilled Him, a little country boy from the
village of Nazareth, when He saw it for the first
time at the great feast. He seems to have had
no fear, as with all simplicity He pressed near
to the great doctors of learning, listening eagerly
and asking keen questions, the keenest questions that can be asked—those that leap from
the alert and hungry mind of a boy of twelve.

And we read of that other day when He heard
the quarrelings and cursings, saw the gross
wickedness of the bargainings of the money-

changers and those who bought and sold the sacrifices, and cried aloud in words of burning denunciation, ''My house shall be called of all nations the house of prayer but ye have made it a den of thieves!''

Little wonder that the scribes and Pharisees looked aghast at the crowds that pressed to hear as He taught daily in the temple, or that they demanded by whose authority He did these things and asked each other helplessly what they could do, since ''the people were very attentive to Him,'' and ''the whole world had gone after Him.'' In the temple courts how keen were His answers to their clever questioning designed to condemn Him, so keen that after awhile none dared ask Him any more questions. Yet when the teaching was over and, leaving the half-hostile, half-admiring crowd, He went out to the Mount of Olives to pray—then He knew that He must die.

It all seemed very real as we sat looking down upon the City. So real that we dreaded to read of the days before Him, of the hard way that the rulers of the synagogue, because of their jealous conservatism, the desire to make their own places secure, the fear lest the people should follow Him as prophet and leave them as priests, had already in their hearts condemned Him to go. So we closed the Book.

Leaving the carriage again at the Damascus Gate we wandered back past the convents, through Christian Street. The city was becoming a very live thing to us. The children smiled at us as we passed through the narrow arcade to our hotel. Oranges and dainty soft spring flowers from the valley were in our room.

"I have lived thousands of years today," said my friend. "I have been fighting all the battles from the days of King David to the days of King George and I am weary." I smiled in sympathy, for one does not live in days or years in Palestine but in centuries. The march of events over broken cobblestones, past walls crumbling with age, catches one in its onward sweep and leaves him breathless as he hurries on from what has been to what is, and from what is to what is to be.

We took up our American mail. The steady tread of history's myriad marchers halted for a moment. The clippings from the papers told us of the wedding of a girl whom we love. Across the top of the clipping was written in the

92

girl's own hand, "Unspeakable happiness. The greatest day of my life!" Names of guests, the most minute details as to flowers and gowns followed. In another clipping we read of the divorce of a girl we had known in school. She had been married twenty years. I remembered the account of her wedding. In the hall we heard laughter. Marie was listening to the extravagant compliments of Alphonse. A letter from a boy of eleven asked for stamps from Egypt and Palestine. "I want them more than anything in the world," he wrote. The next letter brought a clipping making passing reference in six short lines to a critical misunderstanding in the Far East. While we were reading it, a woman came to tell us a story of great sorrow and desperate need. The wild storm of human wrath and revenge that swept over Russia had left her, who had never known anything but love, happiness and plenty, stranded, utterly alone, with not even a ruble of her vast estates.

It is a confusing world. Great events and small jostle each other along its highways. Wrapped securely about with affairs of self, old and young fail to see the momentous hours of human destiny as they pass—pass so swiftly, to leave them on some future day dumb with surprise, aghast at the significance of the things which, having eyes, they saw not and, having ears, they heard not. It is a most confusing and perplexing world, but alas for him who does not love it, pity for him who does not believe in it, shame upon him who will not share the task of saving it.

Tomorrow would be Sunday and we would go to the Garden.

I GO TO THE GARDEN

Who fathoms the Eternal Thought?
  Who talks of scheme and plan?
The Lord is God! He needeth not
  The poor device of man.

I walk with bare, hushed feet the ground
  Ye tread with boldness shod;
I dare not fix with mete and bound
  The Love and Power of God.

Ye praise His Justice; even such
  His pitying love I deem:
Ye seek a King; I fain would touch
  The robe that hath no seam.

Ye see the curse which overbroods
  A world of pain and loss;
I hear our Lord's Beatitudes
  His prayer upon the Cross.

                    —John G. Whittier.

I GO TO THE GARDEN

L IGHT clouds hung over the city that Sunday morning when we looked out at the tower of David, one of the oldest monuments of Jerusalem, standing directly across the open space in front of our balcony. It still looks the part it long played as a watch-tower and a place of refuge and strong defense. The people call it the Citadel, and until the coming of the British it served as a garrison for Turkish soldiers. During our first days in Jerusalem we had walked about Mount Zion, had read of the various controversies waged over exact locations, had gone into the House of Caiaphas, the House of Annas, and had looked at the upper room. They may or may not have been the exact spots made tragic or sacred by that last week of the Great Life. It did not matter to us. The stone courtyards, the little chapels, the marks of Crusaders' crosses, the burial stones made us conscious indeed of the triumphs and tragedies of men and nations that had written

themselves from that hilltop into the history of
Palestine and so into the making of the world.
It was very easy, standing in that upper room,
bare now save for an ancient picture, to imagine
the long table, the couches, the reclining disciples. One is almost overwhelmed as he real-
izes the effect of that simple supper of bread
and wine upon the characters of succeeding generations of men. What breaks in the ranks of
Christendom the varied interpretations of its
significance have made! To what heights of
spiritual power, to what depths of shame, sorrow and repentance has it led those who, following His request, have celebrated it in remem-
brance of Him. In wonderful cathedrals, in
rude chapels, in the lonely spots of earth, in the
jungle, in the desert, on the islands of the sea,
in the hospitals, in prison, on the fields of war
kneeling before improvised altars within sight
of the no man's land which tomorrow would be
their graves, men have heard the words: "As
oft as ye eat this bread and drink this wine—"

How intensely He struggled, in those hours in
the upper room, to make them understand that
He loved them, to lead them to a comprehension
of the meaning of service, to help them to accept

Out there on the wind-swept hills, without priest or altar, we could better understand the words of the Book.

the great commission His death would leave them to fulfil.

We could almost hear the voice of our Lord saying: "Behold the hour cometh, yea is now come, that ye shall be scattered every man to his own and shall leave me alone: yet—I am not alone because the Father is with me.

"These things have I spoken unto you that in me ye might have peace. In the world ye shall have tribulation, but be of good cheer. *I have overcome the world.*"

It was easy to see Peter standing by the fire in the place which they showed to us and to hear the cowardly words, "I never knew him," but easier still, as though a beam of light had fallen upon a dark picture, to hear Jesus saying, "Tell my disciples *and Peter.* . . . Peter, lovest thou me? . . . Peter, feed my sheep."

From the background of Mount Zion we went to the Garden, not to the formal garden of Latin or Greek, with their chapels, their neat little gardens, their oranges and their olive trees planted about with fragrant flowers and green grass, though they are very beautiful, terraced there upon the steep sloping hillside. We went instead to the Armenian Garden, kept as nature made it, a wall with the vine leaning over it, a fallen trunk covered with dull moss, and the olive trees, large and small, gray green with twisted boughs ages old, grass as in a meadow, with lilies of the field nodding here and there in sunny spaces, though it was still winter. A soft mist hung about the hill and settled in low lines over the Garden. In one of the trees, hugging a branch, was a tiny gray bird. We could hear its song in the silence.

The friend who had come with us had been often in the Garden. He told us of the beautiful service of the Relief Workers here on Easter morning, of the night after Allenby entered Jerusalem when the workers filled with joy over the manner of the victory came to this sacred spot to pray in gratitude and for strength for the long wearying days of toil which lay ahead. He told us of the Armenian girl, kneeling early one morning in the damp grass, trying to repeat Gethsemane's prayer. She was a graduate of the American Woman's College, was teaching in a girls' high school when deportation orders came, and from then until her rescue had been an Arab's slave in his dirty tent.

It was very still. The walls of the city shut

100

out its sounds, and it was too early for regular traffic along the road to Bethany. A British Tommy climbed over the wall and sat upon a great rock under a gnarled old tree, his hat in his hand. Pictures of the old masters painted on walls of cathedrals, hanging in great galleries, hymns tender and sweet that had thrilled the souls of thousands, poetry that had comforted man in his deepest hours of need, shadowy forms of Crusaders who had dared the perils of sea and land, hunger and thirst and the swords of the enemy, the monk, the pilgrim, the student searching for truth:—all these passed before us under the olive trees and went out into the mist.

Suddenly the day seemed to fade and that night of centuries ago came stealing into the Garden. Kneeling there under the olive trees, we saw Love make its supreme sacrifice and were not ashamed of the overwhelming emotion that stirred our souls to greater depths than ever had been touched before. We read the words softly—"if possible—if possible—nevertheless thy will be done." The rest of the picture was not so hard to look upon for He had triumphed. He rose from His prayer a *Conqueror*.

101

There was more than one grassy hollow near
the sheltering wall where the disciples might
have slept in the open, as did many at the time
of the Passover. Regretful, He wakened them.
The Roman soldiers with staves and smoking
torches were coming down over the hill. His
doom was sealed. What the law gave them no
right to do, misunderstanding, cunning, and
craft had done. Judas kissed him. We read
the rest of the story from a little book that made
it very plain.[1] Then we prayed, but not with
words—there were no words.

On the little bridge that crosses over the
Kedron to the Bethany road we stood for a long
time looking back, loathe to leave. We remembered the white crosses of yesterday standing in
long rows over there on the other side of the
mount. He was not alone in the Garden! With
Him there had gathered through the centuries
an understanding multitude, young and loving
life as did He, who had met their own Geth-
semanes and gone out from them bravely to die.

Again we went through St. Stephen's Gate
and along the path where the Roman guards had
ied their prisoner. We stopped at Pilate's Hall.

By an Unknown Disciple—Hodder and Stoughton.

102

Like a king indeed he met the false testimony of his accusers, the cynical questions of Pilate, the jesting soldiers who had seen many a man condemned to die but none who met the madness of a multitude that cried "Crucify! Crucify!" with such dignity and calm. No wonder Rousseau cried aloud as he studied the story, "Socrates died like a philosopher, but Jesus died like a God!" With what ardent devotion have the great artists of the past attempted to paint for us those scenes. So vivid were they as we stood there in Jerusalem, looking up at the tower of Antonius where Jesus suffered the scourging, that their reality pierced our souls.

When the fickle crowd left the hall shouting curses as they had shouted hosannas, they moved along the narrow street which still bears the name Via Dolorosa.

Opposite the Pretorium is a convent. In it are orphans and stray waifs picked up about Palestine. The ravages of war have added to the usual number and the place is crowded. On this Sunday they were at service, and the clean happy faces as they sang made us feel that it was because of the Sorrowful Way over which He had walked that they were sheltered and fed.

103

Although intended for Jews, Turk and Armenian, Jew and Gentile sat together in the Chapel of Love and Forgiveness. It is under this convent, many feet below the level of the present street that one finds bits of the old Roman pavement over which the multitude, curious, cruel, mocking, followed Him to the place of crucifixion.

Each spot along the Via Dolorosa is marked —the place where the Master took up His cross, the turn in the narrow street where in answer to the tears and prayers of the women He said, "Daughters of Jerusalem, weep not for me, but weep for yourself and your children," the spot where, staggering from weakness, He fell beneath His cross and Simon lifted it and carried it to the hill of Death, dumbly sharing the Saviour's pain. At each place of suffering as we passed, we saw men and women praying and making the sign of the cross. All men walked silently.

Via Dolorosa, since the coming of the British, is scrupulously clean. The houses of stone with beautiful doorways and old carvings on the doorposts make a solid unbroken wall on either side, and very early the street is quite dark. Narrow and not even a mile in length, it stands out in the memory above all the great highways of the world.

We did not follow the narrow streets to the Church of the Holy Sepulchre where reverent worshipers were at that moment kneeling before the tomb, or kissing the stone upon which are the marks of the three crosses. It seemed incredible to us at first that this small church could cover both the spot which was called Calvary and the tomb in the garden of Joseph of Arimathea. Within the church are the chapels of the Greeks, the Romans, the Armenians and the Copts. In each are beautiful shrines with very precious lamps studded with jewels, lamps that burn in honor of each of the four Christian groups. Once there were four great doors of entrance to the Church of the Holy Sepulchre, but so frequent were the quarrels of those coming to worship that these doors were closed leaving only one way of entrance. The key to this door is still held by a Mohammedan according to the command of General Allenby, in memory of the fact that the Caliph Omar spared and continually protected this Church. Priceless jewels are hidden within it, the gifts of Pilgrims from every land. Its treasury is the richest in the world. Jamil saw it when it was shown to the former German Emperor for whom he interpreted, but could never find it again, so devious were the ways that led to it. The Kaiser's gift, presented as with impressive ceremony he knelt to pray, was of great value— in gold.

But it was not to this church of the Holy Sepulchre with its wonderful shrines, its most sacred associations reaching back into the long past, filled with memories of devout men and women, rich and great, poor and lowly, young and strong, weak and old, who had reverently worshiped before the rent in the rock, the place where the soldiers parted His garments, the tomb in the solid stone down in the very bowels of the earth, worn smooth as glass by the feet of pilgrims who, like Peter and John, must stoop to enter it, and Golgotha, reached by winding steps cut in the rock and leading up almost to the roof of the church—it was not this place which we sought as we came from the garden of Gethsemane, following Him along the Sorrowful Way. It was out on the hills beyond the Damascus Gate to the spot called Gordon's Calvary that we went, not because we cared to enter into all the reasons why many believe it to be the place of suffering, rather than the other, but because out there on the wind-swept rocks under a darkening sky, with a garden in the little valley and the tombs cut in solid rock, their "great stones" lying near—out there with no priest and no altars it was easier to read the words of the Book and try to understand them.

It was on this Mount of Calvary, looking down upon the city, that there came to us an overwhelming sense of the sin of selfishness and greed. In the ruins of Belgium we had felt it, in the tumult of war on the battle-fields of France we had seen what it could do, in the records of the desperate struggles of the Peace Table we had caught glimpses of its power, in China we saw its work, in Korea we looked upon its suffering victims, and here on Calvary the weight of the world sorely wounded and dismayed by sin, pressed hard upon us. It would not have been possible to bear had we not read also of the stone rolled away and the great triumphant Victory.

A deep conviction settled down upon us until it possessed every muscle and fiber of body and

107

mind, until it possessed our souls—the thing that He preached and that only can save the world. His great command that man love his God and serve his neighbor—this principle alone can rescue humanity from the abyss of chaos into which blind greed, individual and national, has plunged it. As the pilgrims knelt at the Holy Sepulchre, we knelt there under the open skies on the hill that is called Calvary to accept again His first great commandment, and the second that is like unto it, in repentance and humility to pray for pardon for past failures and strength for new endeavors.

That night at evening service in clear soprano voice a boy in the choir sang:

> There is a green hill far away
> Without the city wall
> Where the dear Lord was crucified
> Who died to save us all.
> Oh dearly, dearly has He loved
> And we must love Him too,
> And trust in His redeeming blood
> And try His works to do.
>
> There was no other good enough
> To pay the price of sin:
> He only could unlock the gate
> Of Heaven and let us in.
> Oh dearly, dearly has He loved
> And we must love Him too,
> And trust in His redeeming blood
> And try His works to do.

108

I Go To The Garden

The echo of the last line followed us home. There is work to be done—challenging, mighty world-building tasks—and for the doing of them those who call themselves servants and followers of Him whose brave, suffering footsteps we had traced from the Garden along the Sorrowful Way to Calvary have waited too long.

I GO DOWN INTO EGYPT

The strings of camels come in single file
  Bearing their burdens o'er the desert sand;
Swiftly the boats go plying on the Nile
  The needs of men to meet on every hand.
    But still I wait
For the messenger of God who cometh late.

                              —Author Unknown.

I GO DOWN INTO EGYPT

IT was sitting on a housetop overlooking Jerusalem on the last day of our visit to the Holy City that we heard in detail the story of the official entry of the British forces. The woman who told us had spent the years of the war as well as most of her life in Jerusalem though she is an American. Her children were born there, she speaks many of its languages, she knows its people and she loves it. She is one of the women appointed by Lord Samuel, the High Commissioner, to serve on an advisory council to assist the government in establishing policies for the protection and betterment of women. She is the Christian representative, the others being Mohammedan and Hebrew.

The story, as she told it, revealing all the fear and anxiety of those hard years, the pressure of uncertainty, the daily, hourly struggle for food with sufficient nourishment to keep the children and the old people alive, made us feel again, as so many times before, the sharp stab of

113

the fact that it is not those who bear arms alone who go to war. Little faces, whose right it is to be round and rosy, covered with smiles, must be pale and wan, yes, must even forget how to smile, as millions of little ones have forgotten since nineteen hundred and fourteen. Old faces, whose right it is to bear the marks of peace and contentment after the struggle of the years, must be left instead with marks of pain and anguish as have millions of the aged since nineteen hundred and fourteen. He is a cruel monster, War, and if man, after what he has seen these past years, does not imprison him, starve him, and leave him to die, then man deserves the bitterness of the fate that will be his.

Threatened deportation, first by the German, then by the Turk, had been again and again postponed for the little group known as the American Colony but finally word came that in ten days all must go. The men of military age, though neutral, had been ordered away a week before and were expecting the arrival of a Turkish officer at any moment, to tell them the time had come. Food was very scarce, there was no sugar, little flour, and no fats. The woman who told us the story was herself doing all-day and

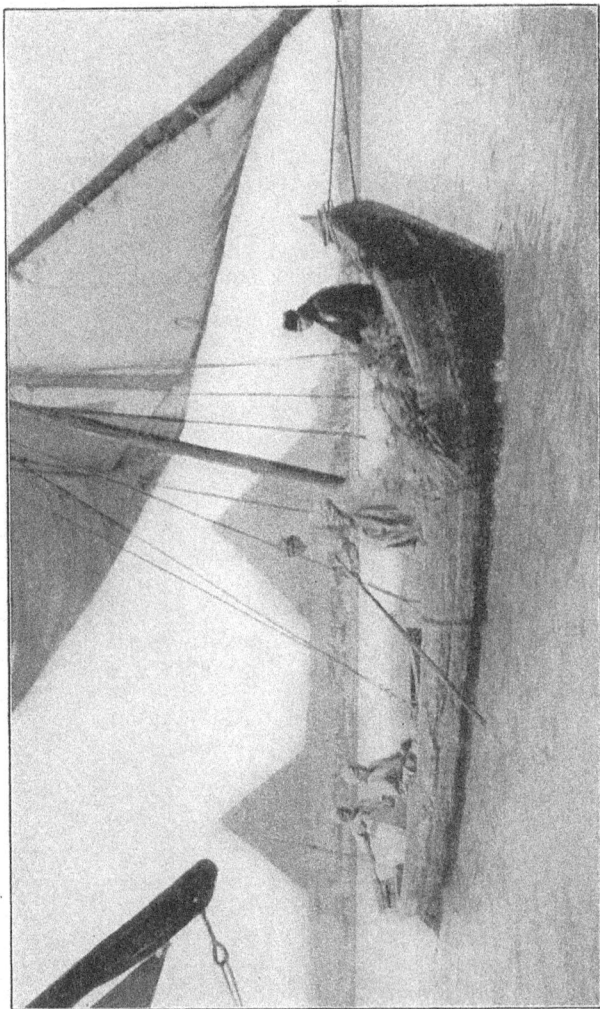

When we opened our eyes, the Nile lay almost at our feet.

sometimes all-night duty as a nurse in the Red Crescent Hospital which was our present hotel. Some of the letters she showed to us proved what a consolation she must have been to the young British soldiers, who lay with the Turks, prisoners, and sorely wounded. The thundering of the guns had been drawing nearer but, despite rumors that crept into the streets and the hospital wards that the Turks were slowly losing ground, they themselves reported progress. Great airplaines droned over the city, cannon roared in the hills. One afternoon there was unusual commotion in the open space before the hotel and, standing by the window, our friend saw the Germans making hurried preparations for leaving. Signal wires, telephone wires, rugs, removable furniture, tons of supplies, went out through the Jaffa Gate. The Turkish General visited her—he must leave the wounded in her care. The German doctors would go with the troops. He would leave two days' provisions and medicines, after that—

When he had gone, half afraid to believe it, she whispered the word to the British patients. They were nearly mad with joy, and there was little sleeping that night. "When? When?"

they would whisper as she or her helper passed
them. She could only answer, "I do not know.
We have provisions for two days." Very early
in the morning, before it was fully light, the
Mayor of the city, one of the direct descendants
of Mohamet, sent her a message saying that he
was about to surrender the city.

At half-past eight that morning the outposts
saw the white flag approaching. General Shea
was the officer sent by General Allenby to accept
the surrender of the city. At half-past twelve
Jerusalem had passed into the hands of the
British, guards were placed at all public buildings, and instructions given to the Chief of
Police. The joy of the people—Jew, Christian,
and Moslem—was shown in the crowds that
filled the street, the tears and embraces, the
shrill cries in many tongues. Even the Turkish
sick and wounded in the hospital showed relief.
For the twenty-third time in its history Jerusalem had surrendered. But this time there were
no cries for mercy, no bitterness, no wailing,
no terrible fear of the conqueror.

Outside the walls the guns banged and hammered at the Turkish defences. Much had to be
done before Jerusalem was safe from attack, but

116

although, spurred on by advices from Germany, the Turks made an attempt to recapture the City, it was a disastrous failure.

One of the young men joined us on the roof and contributed his share of the description of the next thrilling days. It was on December 11th, 1917, that General Allenby, Commander-in-Chief, took formal possession of the City. He would not enter through the break in the old wall made when the former Kaiser with his great retinue entered as a Crusader. Indeed orders have been given to have the break closed. Allenby would carry no flag. On foot and accompanied by a Guard that altogether numbered about one hundred fifty, he stood on Mount Zion on the steps of the Citadel at the entrance to David's Tower. He had been met outside the narrow gate by the Guard representing all branches, faiths and races that make up the British Army. Behind him, as he stood on the steps with his staff, were the leading men of the City, ready to listen to the reading of the Proclamation. There were no shouts of victory, no trumpets, no evidence of the spirit of triumph over a foe. The Proclamation was read in Arabic and English, in Hebrew and Greek, in Russian,

117

in French and Italian. As the people, standing respectfully in the open spaces and upon the housetops, heard each in his own tongue that all men might "pursue their lawful business without fear," and the promise that "every Holy Place, revered and held sacred by any faith, will be defended and protected," a look, first of incredulity, then of confidence, passed over their faces. Many Mohammedans ran from the square to repeat the words in homes from which some fearful ones had not dared to come. Murmurs and gestures of approval were given on every side. The windows of the Red Crescent Hospital were filled with faces of those who, though very ill or badly wounded, could not miss this significant moment of the Great War. All the promises made that day have been sacredly kept, our friends told us.

In the old Turkish barrack square the Commander-in-Chief met the heads of all the religious communities. The sheikhs in charge of the Mosque of Omar, the representatives of the Priests and Patriarchs of the Latin, Greek Orthodox, Armenian, and Coptic churches who had been deported by the Turks, the heads of the Jewish communities, the Syrian Church, the

118

Greek Catholic, the Abyssinian and the Anglican Churches, all were there. It was indeed a cosmopolitan company as to religious faiths. "The bright color of the holiday dress which most of the people had put on, I can see in detail at this moment," said our friend. "Not one step in that simple ceremony shall I ever forget. In two hours, leaving guards over all holy places, with Mohammedan officers and soldiers from the Indian regiments to guard the Mosque of Omar, the General walked back through the Old Jaffa Gate as he had come, received the salute of his troops, entered his car and went down to the fighting area.

The relief workers took up the heavy burden of bringing food to the people whose thin bodies and pale faces showed the effect of months of starvation diet. All supplies must come up over roads muddy and torn by heavy traffic, crowded with army food and equipment that must have right-of-way. The task was one that taxed patience and energies to the utmost. The health commission assumed the equally great task of clearing the streets of unspeakable filth left in the wake of the Turkish rule, our friends shouldered their burden of securing medical atten-

119

tion and food for the sick, helpless and wounded men.

"Only gradually," said our friend walking up and down on the roof, her cheeks flushed by the memories of days so vividly recalled, "did we come to realize that this Holy City was *free*. It was as though we had been going about in heavy chains that, suddenly taken from us, had left us too dazed to move. We unconsciously looked for old restrictions, old threats, old taxes suddenly to be laid upon us. Despite the glory of its past," she added, leaning far over the parapet to look out upon it, "the City in all its long history was never so truly the City of Zion as now."

When we went back to our hotel, standing at the windows from which the wounded had looked, we felt that though other scenes of many cities in many lands would fade with the years, the description of that day when a victorious army under the leadership of a great General, a true soldier, and a Christian gentleman had, beneath the shadow of the Tower, proclaimed a message of possession more truly in accord with the word and teaching of Jesus than any ever recorded in history, would never leave us.

I Go Down Into Egypt

The sunset that night was more glorious than any we had seen. The hills were on fire with it, the Gate was gold. Then the valleys darkened, the streets were still, the crowd of Arab and Greek, Jew and Moslem, the shepherds, the merchant with his camels, the shopmen and the traveler, all sought shelter. It was night, and we looked for the last time out on the hills to the place where the stars shone over Bethlehem. Never did more reluctant pilgrims leave a Holy Place.

The train, going twice each week down from Jerusalem and connecting with the train for Cairo, had begun to carry both sleeping compartments and dining car. We boarded it late that night at the foot of the long hill. Before it was light, we had pulled out of the Jerusalem station and did not get even one more glimpse of the city set on a hill. Instead when we opened our eyes we were almost out of the Judean Hills and soon were moving along through desert-rimmed lowlands. Then the desert itself lay about us for hours, livened by occasional caravans that also were going down to Egypt. Once an airplane flew over us and on into the glare of the cloudless sky. We thought often of

121

Joseph and Mary and the Child fleeing through this lonely desert to find in alien Egypt refuge from the jealous wrath of the Roman king. How rapidly the world has learned to cover time and space since then! How slow has been its progress toward the kingdom the Child, whom Herod feared, had come to build. God grant that now over the new paths through old Palestine messengers bearing Good Will may come with all speed.

At Kantara we saw a company of Jews sent by the Zionists into Palestine. They were a weary group, their faces bore marks of deep suffering. They spoke Russian only, so we could not talk with them. They were going by train to Haifa. We could only hope that their sorrows were over and that in the land of their fathers they would find peace, a chance to forget, shelter, food and a home. But we could not feel sure. The threatening words we had heard from the lips of the Arab, the protests on the part of the Jews that there was not land enough in Palestine capable of bearing crops to give food to those who now struggled to live, the bitter race hatreds and religious feuds very near the surface always ready to burst into flame,—

122

these things made us doubtful. The transformation within a generation of this land of Palestine into a safe and happy home for all the Jews of all the world seems but the futile day dream of children when one faces conditions as they are. Many lands have done many things to the Jew who once in simplicity worshiped the God of Abraham, Isaac, and Jacob and tried sincerely, not only to obey the great commandments of Moses, but to teach them to his children. Whether again they can gather from all lands and bring with them the best who shall say? It may be that the fervent exhortations of rabbis, the wisdom of judges, the training of educators, the science of agriculturists, the modern irrigation miracles of engineers, the proper placing of peoples, will make of Palestine a modern state where the dream of economists, political and social, will one day be demonstrated in action. The only spot we saw that seemed like the coming of the day was Ramallah, the city that had to be taken by storm before the troops could reach Jerusalem and visited by us to see the splendid work of the schools of the Quakers who for long years have given learning and new life to children of Syrian and

123

Armenian, and now and then to a Moslem or a
Jew. From that little town between six and
seven hundred Jews and Syrians had emigrated
to America. Since the war many had returned
and were rapidly building the city. Others had
sent money to rebuild the homes of their fami-
lies. These homes were of stone built two stories high with the flat roof but with plenty of
space for light and air. Gardens surrounded
many of them and trees were being planted
everywhere. The children were well nourished,
well clothed, and well trained. It helped us to
have more confidence in the dreams with the
fulfilment of which all Christendom is in sympathy. If only patience and unselfishness can
be set as watchmen over against the door of
enthusiasm! We were told that the Hebrew
High Commissioner of Jerusalem looks to
Ramallah as a prophecy.

We sat for a while on the journey from Kantara to Cairo with a British officer and a nurse
who had seen hard service during the war and
is now in charge of a number of stations where
the native nurses meet her to report progress
and receive further instructions. She helps
them to understand the care of mothers and

young babies and trains them to fight the terrible diseases of the eye that result in a staggering percentage of blindness. The native girls are taking up their work with enthusiasm, even the little children are sharing in the campaign against flies. ''That is a far harder campaign than any we have ever waged when you consider the people you have to train to fight,'' said the officer. And remembering the flies on our days at Suez and Port Said, we could agree with him. It was nearly midnight when she left the train at a little station in the sand. Her man-servant was waiting with her horse and we watched her ride off to her hospital out there somewhere in the blackness. ''No finer women on God's earth than those who wear that uniform,'' said the officer.

A half hour or more and he left us. He was a lover of the desert and almost made us forget how pitiless, how cruel, how destitute of all that makes life for most of us, it is. He knew the names of all the stars and when they would appear in the velvet sky over his great stretch of camps. He loved the cold of the night and was not afraid of the heat of midday, he loved the sunrise and sunsets and ''the desert-folk

worth many times the puny men of cities.''
He, too, rode off into the darkness.

At last—Cairo—and we left the train through
the long station, bright as day. A car was waiting. The luxury of our room made us feel that
we had entered fairyland. It had been so long
since we had seen the things for rest, comfort
and cleanliness that had in our past been common necessities, that now after these months of
journeying about the world they seemed
extravagances indeed!

The next morning we looked through the open
French windows with their rose hangings, out
upon the Pyramids and the Nile. The river lay
almost at our feet. The beauty of it was intoxi-
cating in the soft light of the rising sun. When
my friend broke the silence she said, "It is
indeed beautiful," then smiling she added
"but,—

> If I forget thee, O Jerusalem,
> Let my right hand forget her skill.
> Let my tongue cleave to the roof of my mouth,
> If I remember thee not,
> If I prefer not Jerusalem
> Above my chief joy. . . .

Awake, awake, put on thy strength; put on thy beautiful
garments, O Jerusalem, the holy city. . . . Shake thyself
from the dust; arise, sit on thy throne, O Jerusalem.—
Peace be unto thee, O Zion.''